Praise for *Conversational Capacity*

"*Conversational Capacity* is one of those rare books that will forever change how you see yourself and the people with whom you work. Read it. Recommend it to your boss, your team, and your friends."
——Jan Wilmott, Director of Leadership Development
at the Royal Bank of Canada

"This book provides a practical roadmap to learning the single most important skill that any leader can and should master. *Conversational Capacity* will change the way you lead and transform your relationships—at work and at home."
——Andy Restivo, President and CEO of Creative Channel Services,
an Omnicom Group Company

"*Conversational Capacity* shows leadership teams how to think actively and adapt quickly. Better yet, the simplicity of the book enables the reader to apply the concepts and ideas in any leadership position."
——Mark Milliner, CEO of Personal Insurance at Suncorp

"Craig Weber has a gift for connecting what it means to build healthy relationships with the nuts and bolts of running an organization. In *Conversational Capacity* he brings a refreshing combination of practical tools, personal examples, and wisdom from having worked with hundreds of leaders over the years. If you are a leader or someone interested in getting better at what you do, *Conversational Capacity* is a must-read."
——Rob McKenna, PhD, Executive Director of the Center for Leadership
Research and Development and author of *Dying to Lead*

"Craig Weber challenges us to think differently about the way we talk to each other. Not since the seminal work of Chris Argyris have I read a book that so well documents the promise and the peril of dialogue. Readers will learn to develop conversational competence with team members and with leaders at all levels. You will learn to become more mindful in difficult situations, appreciate the power of curiosity, and develop ways to experiment, compare, reframe, and reengage with renewed commitment. We need this book, now more than ever. Once you read it, you will want to share it as soon as possible!"
——Frank J. Barrett, PhD, Professor of Management and Organizational Behavior,
Global Public Policy, at the Graduate School of Business and Public Policy,
Naval Postgraduate School, and the author of *Yes to the Mess*

"This book has transformed the way I lead, teach, and facilitate. Weber captures the essence of team effectiveness and provides a well-researched and -tested model that supports the other building blocks of leadership."
——Dr. Tony Herrera, Direct of Partner Development at Schreiber Foods

"Required reading! Improving the conversational capacity of your team and organization is invaluable. These same skills are needed to address the broader issues we face as a society. Get this book! Share it with your colleagues, friends, and family."
—Chris Soderquist, President of Pontifex Consulting
and author of *The Strategic Forum*

"Craig Weber's *Conversational Capacity* works. It works to build an internal culture that allows our organization to focus on the work at hand—without the drama, emotions, and egos that often get in the way of creating a high-functioning organization. It also works when building relationships with funders, stakeholders, and other clients, allowing our team to listen for commonalities and to find areas of true agreement."
—Michele Lueck, President and CEO of the Colorado Health Institute

"Those who aspire to use a conversational process to facilitate and deliver high-impact team results have come to the right place. Having worked with Craig Weber to design training programs for colleagues, I can personally attest to his brilliance in using narratives to capture our attention and emotional intelligence with evidence-based methods to build our conversational skills. With clarity, practicality, and case examples, this book will help you find the sweet spot in any conversation while ensuring a productive outcome."
—Dr. Kathleen Keil, Senior Manager of Learning and Development
at Pfizer Animal Health

"Craig Weber's *Conversational Capacity* reduces organizational fear through a simple, effective technique that increases trust and maximizes creativity. It will help any organization realize new levels of confidence, creativity, and success. The tools within these pages may very well be the most important keys to both change and growth in the twenty-first century."
—Scott Eck, President of Leadership Masters

"We often see the need for collaboration but do not have the tools and skills required to make it happen. Using Craig Weber's techniques to build conversational capacity is exactly what we need in both our professional and personal lives."
—Karen Minyard, PhD, Director of the Georgia Health Policy Center
at the Andrew Young School of Public Policy, Georgia State University

"The ideas in these pages are profound, life changing, and applicable to every area of life. My nonprofit team acquired a new set of skills that increased our capacity to tackle governance, interpersonal relationships, and the future in a dynamic and changing economy. Don't miss this opportunity to learn from a master the tools required to elevate awareness, skill, and discipline to achieve desired—and amazing—results."
—Jane Soderquist, Board Chair of the Upper Valley Waldorf School

CONVERSATIONAL
CAPACITY

CONVERSATIONAL CAPACITY

The secret to building SUCCESSFUL
TEAMS that PERFORM when
the PRESSURE is on

CRAIG WEBER

New York Chicago San Francisco Lisbon London Madrid Mexico City
Milan New Delhi San Juan Seoul Singapore Sydney Toronto

11 12 13 14 15 16 QVS/QVS 22 21 20 19 18

ISBN: 978-0-07180712-8
MHID: 0-07-180712-8

e-ISBN: 978-0-07-180713-5
e-MHID: 0-07-180713-6

This publication is designed to provide accurate and authoritative information in regard to the subject matter covered. It is sold with the understanding that neither the author nor the publisher is engaged in rendering legal, accounting, securities trading, or other professional services. If legal advice or other expert assistance is required, the services of a competent professional person should be sought.

—From a Declaration of Principles Jointly Adopted
by a Committee of the American Bar Association
and a Committee of Publishers and Associations

For Dean Williams,
without whom this book would never have been written

Contents

Acknowledgments

Writing a book is a team effort, and over the years many people have provided support, ideas, inspiration, and advice. No one deserves more credit than Dean Williams, without whom this book would not exist. The most illuminating, provocative, and inspiring educator I've ever known, Dean introduced me to the underlying research that informs *Conversational Capacity*. I just hope I don't embarrass him with what I've done with it. I'm also indebted to Chris Argyris, along with Phil McArthur and Bob Putnam, for their brilliant instruction and wisdom at a pivotal point in my learning. My colleagues, Chris Soderquist and Ruth Maxwell, have been a regular source of wise counsel and heartfelt encouragement, as has the entire "ELP team" (Kim, Chris, Ed, Dan, Rick, and Julie). Tony Herrera has been a source of friendship and support for nearly three decades, and Al Preble has been an invaluable partner in learning. I owe a distinct debt of gratitude to my brother Randy who imparted a steady stream of stellar editorial advice on this project. I also want to thank Jackie Beatty, Toni McCarthy, Kim Armstrong, Greg Whicker, and Hannah Tyndal for providing important help with the manuscript.

I must also acknowledge the major role my clients have played in the formulation of these ideas. There are too many to name them all, but a few deserve a special shout-out: Boeing—specifically my years of work at the Boeing Leadership Center in St. Louis, Missouri; Boeing Defence Australia; Vistage (and TEC-Canada), and the thousands of member CEOs, executives, and chairs with whom

I've worked over the past 14 years; Sense Corp; Creative Channel Services; The Georgia Healthy Policy Center at the Andrew Young School of Policy Studies at Georgia State University, and the Upper Valley Waldorf School.

I also want to thank my agent, Lorin Rees, and my editor, Casey Ebro, and her team at McGraw-Hill. Finally, I have to thank my family—Renee, Jason, and Carl—for their support and patience with this project.

Introduction

As our world grows more interconnected and turbulent, building teams that perform under pressure is an increasingly vital task. But creating such teams is surprisingly difficult. Despite our best efforts, our teams and organizations are plagued by behaviors that are as bad for people as they are for business. In our meetings and mergers, in performance feedback and change initiatives, and when making decisions and solving problems, we suffer from a chronic mismatch between the good we *intend* to achieve and the ways we *work together* to achieve it. In situations that require open dialogue, high collaboration, and learning, we instead get closed-minded debate, zero-sum conflict, and defensiveness. The only groups that regularly benefit from the ensuing dysfunction are pharmaceutical companies, therapists, and bartenders. It's not that we're naive—we know that working in a team will always be a roller-coaster ride. We'd just like to feel that we're riding in the car and not lying on the tracks.

So why are healthy, highly effective teams so hard to create? In the pages that follow, we'll see that putting together teams that perform well in tough circumstances remains a frustrating goal because we overlook the most important piece of the puzzle: *conversational capacity*. If we continue ignoring this critical variable, nothing will work the way we intend. We'll say nothing when we should speak up. We'll quarrel when we should inquire. We'll remain reticent when we should be resolved. We'll be closed-minded and critical when we should be open-minded and curious.

1

But it doesn't have to be this way. It is possible to build more reliably vibrant and adaptive teams, working relationships, and organizations. To this end, I'll outline a proven discipline that allows us to communicate and work together effectively as we engage our most troublesome issues and challenges. This discipline helps build teams that are increasingly healthy, sustainable, and effective: *sustainable* because they're more resilient and learning-oriented, able to successfully adapt in shifting circumstances with greater speed and creativity; *healthy* in that the way the team works together is as good for people as it is for business (no matter what business they're in); *effective* because they can consistently align their intentions and behaviors, and engage their toughest issues with greater confidence and skill.

Unfortunately, we can't just snap our fingers and magically acquire this discipline. We must earn it by making a radical shift in how we think and act as we go about our work. And in our quest to build this discipline we'll be forced to confront the powerful human factors that tear it down. In the pages that follow we see that highly effective teams are hard to build because primal aspects of our nature actually work against teamwork. Along the way, we'll explore some surprising facts:

➤ Getting team members to like, trust, and respect each other—the holy grail of traditional team building—often decreases conversational capacity, severely limiting their ability to work together in difficult circumstances.

➤ Nothing *lowers* conversational capacity more predictably than the presence of authority. This puts executives, managers, and team leaders in a tough bind: charged with building and leading effective teams, their very presence can have the opposite effect.

➤ Human nature is not only the source of the problem; it also provides the solution. By cultivating higher aspects of our nature—candor, courage, curiosity, and humility—we can tame the primal reactions that pull us off center, bolstering our own conversational capacity and that of our teams.

➤ Even more encouraging, I'll show how we can use our daily work experience as an ideal place to practice and build our competence. Armed with this discipline, our teams can respond to tough challenges with greater agility and skill, performing brilliantly in circumstances that overwhelm less disciplined teams.

➤ I'm not advocating a simple gimmick or a quick fix. If we want to build our conversational capacity, we must subordinate our base, ego-driven impulses to finer aspects of our humanity. If we want to improve our teams and organizations, in other words, we have to improve ourselves.

Who Should Read This Book?

As an international consultant specializing in team and leadership development, I've spent the better part of two decades helping an eclectic roster of clients improve their performance by treating dialogue as a discipline. I wrote *Conversational Capacity* for managers, CEOs, executives, HR professionals, consultants, project managers, team leaders, and *anyone* else striving to lead their organizations to higher, healthier, more sustainable levels of performance. Eminently practical, the ideas have been tested and refined in a host of tough organizational settings. They work.

My goal is to put the issue of conversational capacity front and center in the minds of readers and to demonstrate that it's a decisive competence for teams, working relationships, and organizations of all kinds. This is vital, because despite its growing importance, it's not getting the attention it deserves.

Standing on the Shoulders of Giants

To paraphrase Sir Isaac Newton, I'm standing on the shoulders of giants as I present this book. My work sits at the intersection of two paths of inquiry and thought: The first is the brilliant work of Chris Argyris of Harvard and the late Don Schön of MIT. Just as Crick and Watson fundamentally revolutionized our understanding of biology and life processes with their discovery of the double-helix DNA molecule, the social science research of Argyris and Schön has had an equally significant impact on our understanding of people and the organizations they create and maintain.

The cross street at this intersection of thought is the work of Ron Heifetz and Dean Williams, both of the Kennedy School of Government at Harvard. With his first book, *Leadership Without Easy Answers*, Ron brought fresh ideas to a stale subject—the exercise of leadership. In *Real Leadership*, Dean expands on Ron's work and provides helpful detail about the varying kinds of challenges for which leadership is required and specific strategies for making it happen. They have outlined an important and profoundly practical notion of what leadership is, what it isn't, when and where it's needed, as well as how it can be effectively exercised in a wide variety of circumstances.

The ideas in *Conversational Capacity* have been stewing in my mental Crock-Pot for a number of years, and I've drawn on ideas and concepts from a variety of sources, but the overall framework that emerges is something uniquely mine. So while my work sits at the intersection of two impressive bodies of thought and research,

I have cooked up a slightly different take on many of the key ideas and how they connect and interrelate. Any problems with the ideas of Argyris and Schön, or Heifetz and Williams, stem from my attempts at interpreting their work—not from the work itself. I'm not ashamed to admit that if I am even traveling on the same intellectual highway as these turbocharged thought leaders, I'm puttering along in the far-right lane.

It's not just the underlying research that makes the concepts in this book so useful. For many years my ideas have been slammed up against real-world problems and challenges in a wide variety of teams and organizations. From this ongoing interplay between theory and practice evolved an engaging and practical discipline for improving how we participate in teams and organizations. In my work with small businesses, Fortune 10 megafirms, nonprofits, government agencies, educational institutions, and the military, I've seen the damage low conversational capacity produces in a wide variety of organizational contexts. Yet I've also seen individuals and teams who have rolled up their sleeves and worked hard to use the ideas outlined in this book to improve their performance by bringing more mindfulness and discipline to how they communicate and work with one another.

Where Do We Go from Here?

What do I mean by conversational capacity, and why is it an issue? Why aren't we naturally good at talking about any issue without getting defensive and dysfunctional? In Chapters 1 and 2 we'll answer these questions as we delve into the concept of conversational capacity and the human factors that limit it. In Chapters 3, 4, and 5 we'll then explore a discipline for building our capacity that requires that we think, act, and be different in meetings and conversations.

This discipline is important, because while we spend tremendous effort to *understand* our tendencies and behaviors (with a host of popular personality assessments and various forms of anonymous feedback, for instance), we invest precious little in actually learning to *manage* them. In Chapters 6 and 7 we'll look at two priceless advantages conferred on a team with high conversational capacity, enabling them to perform at an entirely different level than a team that lacks it. Finally, in Chapters 8 and 9 we'll look at strategies for building our discipline as we work day by day, as well as the connection between conversational capacity and team leadership.

It's About Teams

The focus of this book is on improving teams and teamwork, and my definition of team is fairly expansive: A team is any group of people working together in the pursuit of a mutual goal. That includes a finance team in a large company or the faculty at an elementary school, but it could also be the entire company or school. Working in an organization is a team sport. So, for the purposes of this book, any work group, function, project, collaborative working relationship, or enterprise can be considered a team.

How to Use This Book

There is no single occasion for using this book. Read it when you need to build your capacity for robust dialogue around tough issues. Read it, too, when you're moving into pivotal change and want to bolster your ability to manage the tensions and conflicts you'll inevitably face. Turn to it as a resource when your team wants to do some no-nonsense team building and gain tangible, lasting skills in the process. Come back to it whenever you're part of an organization or team that isn't working as well as you'd like.

While you can read *Conversational Capacity* alone, the book will have even more impact if you dig into it with team members, partners, colleagues, customers, and others with whom you work. Treat it like a workbook, a catalyst for thought, discussion, and experimentation. You may not agree with everything you find in its pages. That's fine. Take notes. Do your own research. Kick the book's tires and take its concepts for a test drive. Consider how the ideas, concepts, and stories relate to *your* experience. Have you faced similar problems in the past? Are you facing them now? Make the reading of this book the beginning of an exploration of the ideas, not the end of it.

What Challenges Are You Facing?

I use a variety of examples from the fields of medicine and aviation. I do this not because the problems are more prevalent in these arenas—they're not. I do it because in these fields the consequences of low conversational capacity are so extreme. I'm trying to make a clear distinction, and the stark examples help pull the concepts into sharper focus. The key is to think about how the examples relate to your experience and to the situations and challenges facing you and your team.

Since I'm asking you to think about how the ideas in this book relate to your specific challenges, let me quickly prime the pump by making an important distinction regarding two basic types of problems. The first is what I refer to as a routine problem.[1] Routine problems may be painful, expensive, and frustrating, but we have the advantage of knowing *what* to do about them and *how* to work through them. We have, in other words, a routine for dealing with them.

Contrast a routine problem with an adaptive challenge.[2] An adaptive challenge is a problem for which we have no ready solutions, no expert we can call upon to guide us through, no clear way forward. We have, in other words, no routine. We know we're facing an adaptive challenge when we find ourselves in unfamiliar territory with no mental map of our predicament. Lost in uncharted terrain, we must pull together with the people around us to make sense of the hard realities we're facing and successfully adapt to the new environment.

This is a vital distinction for the subject we're about to explore because the more adaptive the challenge we're facing, the higher the conversational capacity needed to productively engage it. So, as you read the pages that follow, reflect back on these questions: What are the adaptive challenges facing your team? Is the conversational capacity of your team sufficient for dealing with those challenges? If not, how can you and your colleagues bridge the gap?

A Fork in the Road

In the grand sweep of human history, our modern organizations are a recent invention, and we've still got a lot to learn about putting together teams that really work when it counts. The pages that follow provide a critical piece of that important puzzle. They show a way to dramatically improve not just how we communicate, but how we collaborate, influence, manage, and lead.

After you finish reading this book, you'll be a far more astute observer of conversations and meetings, recognizing behaviors you previously failed to notice. But you won't just be more aware. You'll also have a practical set of skills for participating in conversations in a far more balanced, deliberate, effective way. And, if you're willing to practice, you'll get better over time, gradually increasing your conversational capacity and that of your team.

But be warned, this book will present you with a choice. We spend so much time at work, it's bound to affect who we are. The only question is how. Will we let our experience reinforce the primal, self-centered aspects of our nature, or the nobler, more purpose-driven aspects of our humanity? Will we grow more candid or more cautious? More courageous or more timid? More curious or more critical? More humble or more arrogant? Far too many people opt for the lower, easier, less rigorous route. This book will encourage you to take the higher, more adventurous road—the road less traveled.

Conversational
Capacity

THE MISSING PIECE
OF THE PUZZLE

....

Management's business is
building organizations that work

JOAN MAGRETTA

I n elementary school I had a friend named David. One sunny
day at recess, David, an epileptic, fell to the ground in the grips
of a violent seizure. By the time I noticed what was happening,
not only was David in physical distress, he was also surrounded by a
group of students who were laughing at him, calling him names, and
making fun. It was an ugly scene.

Shocked, I raced over with the clearest of intentions—to help
David get through the seizure without injuring himself and to defend him from those kids giving him grief. I knew what to do
and I had every intention of doing it, but as I reached my friend, a
disturbing thing happened: I froze in my tracks. I didn't say a word.
I didn't help my friend.

I didn't know it then, but I had fallen victim to a powerful
dilemma that often causes our intentions and our behavior to part

ways. On the one hand, my goal was to help my friend, but on the other, it was to avoid being ridiculed and criticized. I wanted to speak up and help, but I also wanted to remain safe and secure. It's clear now that the latter intention was the more powerful of the two, and that there were two seizures on the playground that day—David's epileptic seizure and my intentional seizure.

At the time I thought it was just me, that I suffered from some unrecognized disability with which most people are unencumbered. Or even worse, I worried that I was simply a coward, too afraid to take a stand for my friend when it counted most. I've since learned that my painful episode on the playground reflects a nearly universal human experience. And, after years of academic study and in-depth work with a wide variety of organizations, I realize my reaction that day was a symptom of a problem affecting all manner of teams and work relationships.

This problem is not just a minor trifle causing mere inconvenience or embarrassment on playgrounds. Its significance is evident in the experience of Colonel Mike Mullane, a weapons and navigational systems officer on a U.S. Air Force F-111 "Aardvark," a fighter-bomber. Early in his career he was on a mission with a pilot with thousands of hours of experience flying this aircraft. When they reached "bingo fuel," the critical point at which there is just enough fuel to return to base, Mullane saw no response from the pilot. Mullane's first instinct was to speak up, to point out that they needed to turn the aircraft around and head home. At risk, after all, was not just their mission and their plane, but also their lives.

But then, like me on the playground, he experienced an intentional conflict. On the one hand, a "little voice" in the back of his brain urged him to raise his concern; on the other hand, he didn't want to be labeled a troublemaker, a non–team player, or a "high-maintenance" flight operations officer. Even worse,

what if he had been misreading the situation and it was not actually bingo fuel? He might've looked ignorant or incompetent.
So despite the obvious danger, Mullane covered up his concern
and said nothing. The consequences were severe. Running out
of fuel on their way back to base, they ejected from the F-111.
Rather than end their mission by landing on a runway as they intended, they instead found themselves swinging under the cano-
py of a parachute as their multimillion-dollar aircraft crashed into
the ground.[1]

Building Teams That Work

These experiences provide a clue to a major problem affecting
teams, team members, and teamwork, a problem that is routinely
overlooked, underappreciated, and, therefore, undermanaged. This
lack of awareness costs us dearly. In our world of mounting complexity and rapid-fire change, there's a growing demand for teams
that work well when the pressure is on. But while we're good at
building teams that perform when facing routine problems, building teams that perform when things get tough remains an elusive
and frustrating goal.

It's not that we haven't been trying. We've been systematically studying how to build more effective and efficient organizations since the late nineteenth century when Frederick Taylor
broke new ground with his time and motion studies, ushering
in a new era of scientific management. But Taylor would barely
recognize the world in which we're working today. Vastly more
complex and interconnected, our world moves in chaotic and unpredictable ways. A torrent of change—technological, economic,
political, and environmental—roars at us with increasing volume
and velocity.

But, while it's more vital than ever to build teams that can thrive in these difficult circumstances, it's clear we're missing something important. Despite the billions of dollars spent every year on strategy formulation, training, restructuring, personality assessments, off-sites, workshops, and all manner of team and organizational development, only 15 percent of mergers and acquisition deals succeed,[2] and executives report a rapidly growing gap between the need for change in their organizations and their ability to effectively orchestrate that change.[3] Research shows that 9 out of 10 strategic initiatives fail to deliver their intended results,[4] and among executives who believe they have the right strategies in place, only a small fraction feel they are implementing them effectively. As Lawrence Hrebiniak puts it, "making strategy work is more difficult than strategy making."[5]

Not only are our teams routinely ineffective, they're often inhumane. Research shows that working and getting ahead in a wide range of teams and organizations results in "various disturbances—genuine emotional conflicts—that range from mild distress to feelings of self-betrayal, to stress and burnout, to acute psychiatric symptoms and irrationality."[6] Teamwork, it turns out, can be hazardous to our health.

Our efforts to build reliably effective teams yield such poor results because our focus is overly technical. While we espouse our allegiance to the human side of the enterprise, our actions reveal different priorities. We're far more likely to focus our attention and resources on strategy, structure, systems, policy, process, and procedure, delegating the "softer" people stuff to HR, training, or outside consultants. But this overly technical focus is a costly mistake. If we want to build reliably effective teams and working relationships, we need to manage the human side of the enterprise with the same level of rigor and discipline with which we manage the technical.

Conversational Capacity

If we want to build healthier, more capable teams we must pay far more attention to a key piece of the puzzle on which every other aspect of teamwork depends. I refer to it as *conversational capacity*. Put simply, conversational capacity is the ability to have open, balanced, nondefensive dialogue about tough subjects and in challenging circumstances. A team with high conversational capacity can keep its performance on track, productively addressing even its most difficult and contentious issues. But when a team has low conversational capacity, even a petty disagreement can throw team members off balance and derail their performance.

I use the term *balance* to describe a team with high conversational capacity because it provides a useful way to think about the concept. There is a "sweet spot" in any meeting or conversation where the dialogue is open, balanced, and nondefensive. Good work gets done here. While it's easy to remain balanced when talking about routine and comfortable issues, when a difficult subject hits the table, our tendency is to move out of the sweet spot toward the extreme ends of the behavioral spectrum. Some people shut down. Others heat up.

The Sweet Spot

We can define conversational capacity, therefore, as the ability to work in the sweet spot in difficult circumstances that would send most people and teams flying out of it. A team with high conversational capacity can stay focused on learning, and do good work, even in difficult situations, because team members don't allow their emotional reactions to pull them off center.

We know we're communicating in an open, balanced, nondefensive way when there is balance between *candor* and *curiosity*. We don't mind sharing our ideas and perspectives, and we're equally interested in exploring the ideas and perspectives of others. When we're talking about easy subjects, such as how we spent our weekend or a movie we recently watched, it's easy to maintain this balance. But when there's a conflict, a hard decision, a personality clash, or a difference of opinion, it's easy to lose balance by letting go of one attribute or the other.

If we let our candor drop, for instance, our behavior becomes more cautious—we shut down, cover up our views, water down our concerns, change the subject, or feign agreement. On the other side of the spectrum, when we let go of curiosity, our behavior grows more arrogant and aggressive—we heat up, argue our point, stop listening, and push our perspective at the expense of others. So when I say a team has high conversational capacity, I'm saying it has the discipline to balance candor and curiosity in challenging circumstances that throw less disciplined teams off center.

Where's the Line?

To make this more personal, think about your team. Imagine, for a minute, you and your colleagues have created a prioritized list of the toughest issues you're currently facing—the most unwelcome issue at the top and the least unwelcome at the bottom. Whether you realize it or not, somewhere in that list is a line. It represents the conversational capacity of your team.

Below the line, where the capacity is sufficient, you can remain balanced and do good work. That doesn't mean there isn't conflict or tension. It means that despite it, you're able to explore the issues, make informed decisions, and implement them. Because you're able to maintain balance between candor and curiosity, your

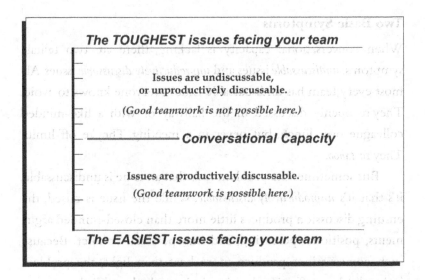

conversations and meetings are productive. Your team's ROC, or *return on conversation*, is high.

When your team tries to address an issue above the line, where its conversational capacity is inadequate, teamwork starts to break down. How could it not? If you try to engage a problem for which you lack the capacity for balanced dialogue, you're in trouble as soon as you start talking. Unable to communicate in the sweet spot, your ROC nosedives in the very circumstances in which you need it to go up.

The tougher the challenge we're up against, the higher the conversational capacity needed to deal with it. So, just as we rate a truck's capacity for carrying a load, we should also pay attention to a team's capacity for dealing with its challenges. If its conversational capacity is too weak given the issues it needs to address, it is, by definition, dysfunctional. The wider the gap between the problems it's facing and its capacity for dealing with them, the greater their incompetence.

Teams and their leaders, therefore, should consider a few vital questions: *Where's the "line" in our list of challenges? Is it high enough? And how can we even tell? What are the warning signs when our capacity for balanced dialogue is low?*

Two Basic Symptoms

When conversational capacity is lacking, there are two telltale symptoms: *undiscussable* issues and *unproductively discussable* issues. Almost every team has undiscussable issues everyone knows to avoid. They're openly discussed in the hallway or with a like-minded colleague over lunch, but never in a meeting. They're off limits. They're *taboo*.

But sometimes the problem isn't that an issue is undiscussable, it's that it's *unproductively discussable*. While the issue is raised, the ensuing discussion produces little more than closed-minded arguments, positional posturing, and interpersonal conflict. Because such conversations produce more heat than light, the problem isn't solved, an effective decision isn't reached, and little progress is made. This means the issue is raised again in a subsequent meeting, or it merely changes status, becoming the newest item on the team's list of undiscussables—another taboo subject everyone knows to avoid.

Nothing Else Compensates for Low Conversational Capacity

These symptoms—*undiscussable* and *unproductively discussable* issues—provide a clear signal that the conversational capacity of a team is inadequate. They're important signals to recognize because, as we're about to see, no amount of technical sophistication or good intentions will compensate for a team's inability to balance candor and curiosity under pressure. Even if a team is staffed with skilled people who trust, like, and respect one another, and even if they have all the technical pieces in perfect place—strategy, structure, processes, and policies—the team still won't perform if its conversational capacity is too low.

This is a bold claim, so let me provide a few examples to illustrate the point. As you read them, see if you recognize anything that relates to your past experience, or even to something you're in the middle of right now.

Proper Structure Is Never Enough

The research of Jeffrey Sonnenfeld, an expert on corporate governance and a distinguished professor at the Yale School of Management, shows that most spectacular board failings, including Enron, Tyco, and WorldCom, were not caused by the lack of structure, process, or policy. In fact, these boards *had* conformed to "most of the accepted standards for board operations," says Sonnenfeld. "Members showed up for meetings; they had lots of personal money invested in the company; audit committees, compensation committees, and code of ethics were in place; the boards weren't too small, too big, too old or too young," he points out. "In other words, they passed the tests that would normally be applied to ascertain whether a board of directors was likely to do a good job."[7] Despite having all these technical aspects in place, however, many boards still fail miserably.

Now, to be fair, it's not an easy role to perform. Among other things, a board defines a high-level mission and purpose; hires a CEO and holds her accountable for performance; maintains fiscal accountability; questions and approves budgets; and governs the organization through high-level policies, guidelines, and objectives.

In order to perform this role well, productive conflict and a willingness to disagree, publicly and rigorously, need to be an integral part of a board's operating culture. "Bonds among board members," says Sonnenfeld, need to be "strong enough to withstand clashing viewpoints and challenging questions." The levels of trust, respect, and candor should be high. The list of undiscussables should be low.

But, in an alarming number of boards he's studied, Sonnenfeld finds just the opposite; a range of defensive dynamics driven by board members' inability to deal with the tough issues they're facing. Some boards go tribal, breaking into "divisive, seemingly intractable cliques." In a clear sign that candor is lacking, some board members use back channels and hallway conversations to bypass the CEO, while others obsessively avoid conflict by steering clear of contentious subjects, feigning agreement, and deferring decisions to other board members. "I'm always amazed at how common group-think is in corporate boardrooms," says Sonnenfeld. "Directors are almost without exception intelligent, accomplished, and comfortable with power—but if you put them into a group that discourages dissent, they nearly always start to conform."

The solution is not technical. "Over time, good-governance advocates have developed no shortage of remedies for failures of governance," he says, but "most of these remedies are structural: They're concerned with rules, procedures, composition of committees, and the like, and together they're supposed to produce vigilant, involved boards. However, good and bad companies alike have already adopted most of those practices." So, if getting the technical aspects of a board in place isn't the answer, what is? "We need to consider not only how we structure the work of a board," argues Sonnenfeld, "but also how we manage the social system a board actually is." When it comes to effective board governance, improving how members communicate and interact is the decisive variable. "The key isn't structural," says Sonnenfeld, "it's social."

Good Relationships Are Never Enough

Relationships based on trust, loyalty, and respect—the holy grail of most team building endeavors—are no guarantee of high conversational capacity, and, perhaps more surprisingly, they can actually harm it. In fact, if their capacity is high, a team can work effectively in the sweet spot even if its members don't like one another personally. A team with weak capacity, on the other hand, will often fly out of the sweet spot under stress even when its members like, trust, and respect one another.

An executive team at a high-tech firm in Silicon Valley learned this lesson the hard way. Growing rapidly and gearing up for a high-profile initial public offering, the executive team needed open, balanced, nondefensive conversations to manage the onslaught of change besetting the business. The team members knew that their casual, "solve problems in the hallway" culture wouldn't scale, and they openly acknowledged the need to build a more mature, sophisticated enterprise.

Their lack of conversational capacity, however, made the transition difficult. The main problem: the place was just *too nice*. Warm, close relationships had been established in the early years of the firm, and the organization's laid-back, friendly culture made disagreement and conflict unwelcome.

In a series of interviews I conducted for their new CEO, every executive raved about how well the team members got along. They all genuinely liked each other. Trust was high. In addition to being nice people, they each brought an impressive depth of knowledge and experience to the team, so the personal and professional respect they had for one another was abundant. The vice president of human resources described the team's "collegial atmosphere." The plain-speaking vice president of marketing summed it up less formally: "The thing I like most about this team," he said, "is that there isn't a single asshole on it."

But this collegiality came at a cost: their nice culture created a bad business. While the team members enjoyed pleasant meetings and warm relationships, they sacrificed the candor needed for rigorous problem solving and decision making in order to maintain the amiable environment. Lacking the capacity for open, balanced, nondefensive dialogue, they avoided many of the tougher issues they were facing. Ironically, the barrier to openness wasn't that members of this team *didn't* get along; it was the fact that they *did*. This demonstrates the difference between liking and respecting each other and the ability to work together effectively when the pressure is on. As the marketing VP put it, "We have all sorts of problems we need to talk about. But no one wants to bring them up. No one wants to become the team's *first* asshole."

Technical Expertise Is Never Enough

Even a team of bright, experienced, technically skilled people will perform dismally if conversational capacity is in short supply. With so much at stake, the field of aviation is rife with examples that demonstrate how true competence requires far more than just technical aptitude. Consider this grim incident shared by the psychologist Cordelia Fine:

> On December 1, 1993, Express II Airlines Inc./Northwest Airlink flight 5719 to Hibbing, Minnesota, descended too steeply, missing the runway altogether. Everyone on board was killed. The cockpit voice recording revealed that the copilot knew that the plane was at too high an altitude for the descent. "Just . . . you just gonna stay up here as long as you can?" was his single tentative attempt to alert the captain to his error. Even as the plane was brushing the tree tops, moments before the crash, the copilot was deferentially answering the captain's questions.[8]

Technically astute enough to recognize a disastrous mistake was being made, the copilot was nevertheless unable to raise his concern with enough force to address the error. In his popular book

Emotional Intelligence, Daniel Goleman provides another disturbing example of how low conversational capacity on the flight deck of a commercial aircraft led to catastrophe:

> *Melburn McBroom was a domineering boss, with a temper that intimidated those who worked with him. That fact might have passed unremarked had McBroom worked in an office or a factory. But McBroom was an airline pilot. One day in 1978 McBroom's plane was approaching Portland, Oregon, when he noticed a problem with the landing gear. So McBroom went into holding pattern, circling the field at high altitude while he fiddled with the mechanism. As McBroom obsessed about the landing gear, the plane's fuel gauges steadily approached the empty level. But his copilots were so fearful of McBroom's wrath that they said nothing, even as disaster loomed. The plane crashed, killing ten people.* [9]

Technically competent but conversationally challenged, this flight crew was also incapable of dealing with a life-threatening situation when it counted. "Today the story of that crash is told as a cautionary tale in the safety training of airline pilots," Goleman explains. "In 80 percent of airline crashes, pilots make mistakes that could have been prevented, particularly if the crew worked together more harmoniously. Teamwork, open lines of communication, cooperation, listening and speaking one's mind—rudiments of social intelligence—are now emphasized in training pilots, along with technical prowess." [10]

Surely these are a couple of rare incidents, right? Sadly, the answer is no. The National Transportation Safety Board, the entity responsible for investigating civil aviation accidents in the United States, estimates that 25 percent of aviation accidents occur because someone doesn't speak up when a mistake is being made.[11] Conversational capacity is a big deal in aviation. When candor gives way to caution on the flight deck of an aircraft, people can die.

It's not just a problem in aviation. The same disturbing gap between technical expertise and conversational capacity is a grave concern in another field where lives are on the line—the practice of medicine. "I met Sorrel King, whose 18-month-old daughter, Josie, had died at Hopkins from infection and dehydration after a catheter insertion," says Dr. Peter J. Pronovost, the medical director of the Quality and Safety Research Group at Johns Hopkins Hospital in Baltimore and a leading expert on hospital safety. "The mother and the nurses had recognized that the little girl was in trouble. *But some of the doctors charged with her care wouldn't listen.* So you had a child die of dehydration, a third world disease, at one of the best hospitals in the world."[12]

In medicine as in aviation, the underlying problem isn't the lack of technical ability; it's the way people communicate. "As at many hospitals, we had dysfunctional teamwork because of an exceedingly hierarchal culture," Pronovost says. "When confrontations occurred, the problem was rarely framed in terms of what was best for the patient. It was: 'I'm right. I'm more senior than you. Don't tell me what to do.'" Pronovost argues that "in every hospital in America," people die because of this very problem. His research into incidents that generated liability claims led him to this sobering question: "In how many of these sentinel events did someone know something was wrong and didn't speak up, or spoke up and wasn't heard?"

His concern is not merely the product of his academic research:

Even I, a doctor, I've experienced this. Once, during a surgery, I was administering anesthesia and I could see the patient was developing the classic signs of a life-threatening allergic reaction. I said to the surgeon, "I think this is a latex allergy, please go change your gloves." "It's not!" he insisted, refusing. So I said, "Help me understand how you're seeing this. If I'm wrong, all I am is wrong. But if you're wrong, you'll kill the patient." All communication broke down [emphasis mine]. *I couldn't let the patient die because the surgeon and I weren't connecting. So I asked the scrub nurse to phone the dean of the medical school, who I knew would back me up. As she was about to call, the surgeon cursed me and finally pulled off the latex gloves.*[13]

High Commitment Is Never Enough

Having a shared set of goals to which a team is highly committed does not inoculate the team against the ravages of low conversational capacity. Social workers in a rough inner-city neighborhood nearly destroyed the very agency they were committed to building despite their fervent dedication to their cause. The team members had grown up in the lively, often abrasive culture of the community they were trying to serve, and when they disagreed with one another, the results were incendiary. Their weekly team meetings were full of caustic exchanges, replete with name-calling, rude insults, and foul language. The more aggressive their meetings became, the more their performance fell. "Adding case-load to this team is like adding fuel to a raging fire," said one exasperated social worker. "The busier *we* get the worse the *meetings* get."

In addition to their deep commitment to their community and their genuine desire to make a difference, these social workers brought a great deal of courage to their roles, regularly walking into neighborhoods and buildings their local police force wouldn't enter without a SWAT team. But, despite all this commitment and courage, they were so afraid of their caustic team dynamic they *sabotaged* the very agency they were committed to building. "When someone comes to our agency with a referral," explained one member of the team, "we often pass it on to a competing agency in the area. No one wants to add more fuel to the fire."

A Good Strategy Is Never Enough

With the help of an expensive, top-shelf consulting firm, the executive team at a financial services company devised a strategy that hinged on increasing the integration and collaboration among previously autonomous business units in order to "cross sell" to customers. The potential gains in revenue were impressive, and the entire executive team agreed that in order to remain competitive this new approach was vital. As far as its strategic intentions were concerned, they were perfectly aligned.

But implementation proved more troublesome than expected. Things quickly bogged down as people, including the executives themselves, resisted the kinds of sacrifices and changes needed to improve integration and collaboration. No one wanted to give up his or her power, influence, customs, or practices, and as a result, the strategy floundered. "I am all for change and sacrifice," the executives seemed to be thinking, "as long as it's everyone else who is doing the changing and the sacrificing." When it became obvious that the strategy was in trouble, the blaming and stonewalling intensified, turbocharging the bunker mentality and intergroup dysfunction that was stifling collaboration and integration.

This executive team spent a small fortune developing its strategy but invested no time or money developing the company's capacity to implement it. Get the strategic intentions right, the team's leaders mistakenly assumed, and implementation will be a snap. This faulty assumption produced a downward spiral of dysfunction. Implementing the strategy took months longer than anticipated, cost far more money than projected, and provided far less competitive value than they'd envisioned.

It's a Pervasive Problem

As these examples demonstrate, when conversational capacity is too low, well-intentioned people behave like a drunk driver who intends to stay on the road but, because his coordination is off kilter, drives into a ditch instead. Like me on the playground or Mullane in the plane, our intentions and our behavior quickly part ways. We remain silent when we should speak up. We argue when we should cooperate. We downplay our concerns when we should blurt them out.

In our day-to-day lives the consequences of anemic conversational capacity may not be so extreme, but they are pervasive. They impact every process and activity that owes its effectiveness to unfettered dialogue and accurate information. Take meetings, for example. We spend a lot of precious time in meetings, and yet most people say their meetings are a big waste of time. Intended to be a vital way of coordinating, sharing information, and dealing with decisions and problems, meetings are rendered woefully inefficient, if not downright useless, when conversational capacity is in short supply.

"I've got a room full of highly paid, intellectually gifted people with the best experience in our industry," a frustrated engineering executive at a large aerospace firm told me. "But we sit in our weekly meetings politely listening to status reports. There's little discussion and no debate." He knew there were real concerns in the room because after meetings all manner of discussion and debate would erupt in the hallways. "But when I express my frustration that no one's talking, all I get are blank stares, and the next meeting the problem is worse," he said. "To be honest, it makes me mad. I went out of my way to hire the best and the brightest people I could find, but I'm not getting access to all the intellectual firepower I'm paying for."

This problem goes well beyond meetings. If we can't have reliably effective conversations about difficult subjects, the basic foundation of our teams, work relationships, and organizations breaks down. We can't solve a problem we can't productively discuss. We can't make informed decisions if the conversations that precede them are riddled with defensiveness and distortion. We have no hope of orchestrating effective change if our ability to deal with the inevitable stresses, tensions, and trade-offs is low. We can't provide useful, responsible performance feedback if we're unable to clearly say what needs to be said. And even if we formulate a brilliant strategy, we have little hope of implementing it if our ability to manage the process is lacking.

The Essence of Teamwork

Conversational capacity should be flashing bright red on the dashboards of everyone responsible for building effective teams and working relationships. This red alert is needed because the subject of conversational capacity is routinely underappreciated, if not completely ignored. When putting together a team we typically don our MBA hats and focus on strategies, structures, financing, processes, staffing, policies, and procedures. When an effort is made to improve how people interact and communicate, it's often squeezed in between golf and wine tasting at the annual retreat. Treated as a second-tier priority at best, these conversational "soft skills" are like the last guest on a late-night talk show—something we may get to if we don't run out of time.

This neglect is misguided. As the world changes with more speed and complexity, teams of every kind need the abilities to address challenging issues with greater balance, focus, and discipline. Conversational capacity is indispensable in building such teams. "An organization is a community of discourse," says Robert Kegan, a developmental psychologist at Harvard. "Leadership," he adds, "is about shaping the nature of the discourse." A *person* with high conversational capacity can do just that. He's able to remain open-minded, non-reactive, and fully engaged in tough circumstances that send his less disciplined colleagues into a highly reactive state of mind. Balancing candor and curiosity, he converses with his teammates in a way that actually increases the conversational capacity of the entire group.

Now imagine a team full of such people. They're able to work together effectively under challenging conditions that trigger most teams into a frenzy of dysfunctional dynamics. They're more nimble, able to identify and correct errors and adapt to changing circumstances far more rapidly than a less-disciplined team. Their conversations are less ego-driven and more purpose-driven: they speak up when they should speak up, and listen when they should listen. They seek understanding when there is a conflict or disagreement, deliberately balancing candor and curiosity, no matter how challenging the circumstances.

When it comes to teams that work well under pressure, this pivotal competence separates the wheat from the chaff. I'd much rather work on a team with high conversational capacity and a flawed strategy, for example, than on a team with low conversational capacity and a perfect strategy. Why? The team with high conversational capacity is able to correct a flawed strategy and implement a new one far more efficiently and effectively than a team lacking conversational capacity can ever implement a perfect one.

In this sense, conversational capacity isn't just another aspect of teamwork—*it defines it*. A team that cannot talk about its most pressing issues isn't really a team at all. It's just a group of people that can't work together effectively when it counts.

The Solution

Sounds simple, right? In addition to getting the technical stuff right, all a team has to do is boost its conversational capacity and all will be well. Unfortunately, it's not that easy.

For starters, we can't just go online and order a fresh box of conversational capacity. It's not something we can purchase, import, or outsource, and it can't be faked, mandated, or coerced. If it's lacking, the only way to get more of it is to roll up our sleeves and build it. The distinct advantages conferred on a team with high conversational capacity must be earned.

But in our quest to earn this capacity we face a formidable obstacle: human nature. In the next chapter, we'll explore two primal aspects of our emotional programming that work against our need for balanced, nondefensive dialogue in difficult circumstances. These deep-seated tendencies trigger knee-jerk reactions that send us flying out of the sweet spot, and if we don't learn to recognize and manage the power they have over our behavior, we'll continue to build teams that function well when things are easy but work poorly when things gets tough.

Fortunately, there's hope. In the chapters that follow I'll share a powerful discipline—a veritable *conversational martial art*—for bridging the insidious gap between our good intentions and our habitual reactions, empowering us to balance candor and curiosity when it counts. This discipline enables a team to reach new levels of performance by members working together brilliantly in circumstances that incapacitate less-disciplined teams. It breathes fresh life into the team's most challenging activities, from continuous improvement to lean initiatives, from strategy implementation to orchestrating change.

As we move forward, I'll describe two game-changing advantages conferred on a team with this discipline. Even better, I'll show you how to use your daily work experience as a dojo, building your skills as you apply them to a range of activities—from problem solving and decision making to meetings and team leadership.

Intentional Conflict

WHY GOOD INTENTIONS
ARE NEVER ENOUGH

....

If we ignore our imperfections on the grounds that
it's too depressing to concentrate on them, then we
greatly limit our future options. On the other hand, if
we know where our limitations are, not just in thinking
but in emotional things. If we know about any hereditary
predispositions we have toward ethnocentrism,
xenophobia, dominance hierarchies, then we have a
chance to moderate those tendencies. If we ignore
any genetic predispositions in those directions, then we
don't make any serious effort to ameliorate them and
we're in much worse shape. This is one of those issues
that every generation has to learn anew, because every
generation has the same hereditary predispositions.

CARL SAGAN

In this chapter, we'll explore an important question: why is
conversational capacity even an issue? Why aren't we naturally
able to talk about any subject without tension or trouble? It's
obviously not something about the issue itself, for two people discussing the same topic can react in very different ways—one finds it

easy while the other does not. No, the problem stems not from the issue or situation, but from us, or, to be more precise, from something in us.

In this chapter we'll learn about the two powerful tendencies that throw us off balance in challenging circumstances, a universal problem that stems from an ingrained aspect of our emotional programming: the fight-or-flight response. When one of these tendencies is triggered, the powerful reactions they spur cause conversational capacity to plummet. To show just how much trouble these tendencies cause, we'll delve into them separately and explore their calamitous impact on teams and teamwork.

Traditional Team Building

Traditional team building focuses on *strategy, structure,* and *relationships*. It's generally believed that if people know *what* they're working together to achieve, understand *how* to work together to achieve it, and *know* and *like* each other well enough, they'll set aside their differences and work together in pursuit of mutual goals. Get the intentions right, it is assumed, and high performance is the inevitable result. But this assumption ignores a critical variable: the conversational capacity of the team. As the last chapter made clear, if a team's ability to work in the sweet spot is too low, it will always underperform. When it comes to effective teamwork, in other words, good intentions are never enough.

Like a feisty Chihuahua that overestimates his chances against the neighbor's pit bull, we overrate the power of our intentions because we assume we have the capacity to communicate effectively about difficult subjects and in challenging circumstances. "We're smart people," we think to ourselves, "We know what to do and how to do it. What could possibly go wrong?" But this optimistic assessment overlooks two hereditary predispositions that often hi-jack our intentions—automatically, and sometimes dramatically. These tendencies often work directly against our other intentions, creating *intentional conflicts*—a clash between opposing objectives in a conversation. If we don't learn to better *recognize* and *manage* these intentional conflicts, we'll continue to build teams that cruise along fine when the road is smooth but break down when the going gets tough.

Mindless Behavior

One reason we have such a hard time *recognizing* the impact these tendencies have on our behavior is that they trigger so mindlessly. They're so well practiced that we no longer consciously notice their effects. It's like driving. I don't have to think about driving my car. I just jump in and go. After years of practice, driving is a predominantly automatic activity. As it is with driving, so it is with many things in life—with enough practice almost any task becomes second nature.

But there's a downside to such highly skilled behaviors. They're notoriously hard to recognize and control, which presents a problem when the mindless reactions that serve us well in one context conflict with our good intentions in another. Chris Argyris refers to this problem—when our mindless reactions work *against* our intentions—as "skilled incompetence."[1] Take something as simple as crossing the street. Every year people are struck by cars because they look the wrong way before stepping off the curb in a foreign country. If traffic comes from the left in their country, they've learned to automatically look left when crossing the street. This skilled response keeps them safe at home, but when they're visiting a country where the traffic comes from the right, this mindless behavior can get them killed. (This very problem nearly changed the course of world events, when, in 1931, while visiting New York, Winston Churchill exited a taxi on Fifth Avenue on the Upper East Side. After looking the wrong way, he stepped into traffic and was seriously injured after being hit and dragged by an oncoming car).[2]

Because these reactions are so automatic it takes tremendous concentration *not* to look the way we've been trained. It's such a problem that in major cities around the globe, the words "Look Right" and "Look Left" are painted on curbs to help visitors from other countries compensate for their habitual tendency to look the wrong way.

Instinctive Behavior

But the mindless nature of the behavioral reactions that knock us out of the sweet spot is not the only problem. They're also exceptionally difficult to *manage* because they're propelled by a primal biological imperative—the fight-or-flight response. When we're hooked by one of these tendencies, we become like the old cartoon character stuck between an angel offering advice into one ear and a devil offering conflicting advice into the other. These conflicting directives come from two parts of our brains that don't always work together in a cooperative, integrated way. One part is older and emotional; the other is newer and rational. The late Carl Sagan explained it so well I'd be remiss not to quote him directly:

> *Feeling, in mammals at least, is mainly controlled by lower, more*
> *ancient parts of the brain, and thinking by the higher, more re-*
> *cently evolved outer layers. A rudimentary ability to think was*
> *superimposed on the pre-existing, genetically programmed be-*
> *havioral repertoires—each of which probably corresponded to*

some interior state, perceived as an emotion. So when unexpect-
edly it is confronted with a predator, before anything like a thought
wells up, the potential prey experiences an internal state that alerts
it to its danger. That anxious, even panicky state comprises a fa-
miliar complex of sensations, including, for humans, sweaty palms,
increased heartbeat and muscle tension, shortened breath, hairs
standing on end, a queasiness in the belly, an urgent need to
urinate and defecate, and a strong impulse either for combat or
retreat *[emphasis mine].*[3]

Our lower brain's penchant for separating our behavior from our higher brain's intentions cannot be overstated. As well practiced as any skills in our behavioral repertoire, these reactions are also turbocharged by instinctive biological impulses. A heritage like this guarantees these reactions will be hard to recognize and even more difficult to control. They turn us into our own worst unintentional enemies because the emotions they provoke lead us to act in automatic ways that violate our otherwise good intentions—we don't help our friend on the playground; we don't confront a pilot making a fatal mistake on a plane; we dismiss the concerns of nurses at the expense of a young patient.

The intense reactions these tendencies trigger hamper our ability to work with, and learn from, people with different points of view, a phenomenon that explains why our efforts at team building so regularly miss the mark. Focused on clarifying, aligning, and improving *intentions,* our efforts to build solid teams ignore a fundamental reality: In difficult circumstances, the good intentions that stem from one part of our brains are often hijacked by the primal reactions from another part of our brains. Any team building that ignores this reality is futile, for it merely clarifies and refines intentions we can't implement when it counts.

Two Troublesome Tendencies

The two tendencies we're about to explore cause conversational capacity to plummet because they send us flying out to the far ends of the behavioral spectrum. One leads us to abandon candor and "flee," the other, to lose curiosity and "fight."

The Sweet Spot

Flight ◄——————— ● ———————► *Fight*

What's more, these tendencies are less likely to cause us trouble in easy, familiar, routine circumstances and far more likely to trigger in stressful, threatening, unfamiliar ones. This means that right when we most need our behavior and our intentions aligned, it's least likely to happen—not because we're stupid, apathetic, or inattentive—but because these primitive reactions make it difficult for us to act consistently with our good intentions.

Given their pivotal impact on our effectiveness, let's look at these tendencies one at a time and explore their impact on conversational capacity.

Flight: When Candor Gives Way to Caution

Imagine you're sitting in a meeting where your team is discussing a major decision about an important project. The rest of the team, including your manager, feels strongly about one particular decision, but you don't agree. As you listen to the way people are thinking, you find you have growing reservations about the direction they're heading. With much at stake, you want to speak up and raise your concern.

But then you experience an intentional conflict. On the one hand, you feel compelled to speak up, but on the other hand, you don't want to cause trouble, be labeled a troublemaker or non–team player, tarnish your reputation within the team, or damage relationships. There's a good chance you don't even consciously recognize the conflict you're experiencing; you just *feel* it. And since the emotional tug of this tendency is so strong, you sit there quietly, covering up your concern, nodding, and feigning agreement. You say nothing. When this happens, you're falling prey to the powerful need to "minimize" the level of negative emotion, tension, or threat in the situation.[4]

When our need to play it safe overwhelms our clear and noble intentions, we sacrifice progress and effectiveness for comfort and safety. We *minimize*.

The Sweet Spot

Minimize ⬅━━━━━━━━ ● ━━━━━━━━➡

It was this tendency that threw me off balance on the playground. On one hand, my intention was to help my friend, but on the other hand, I wanted to minimize my vulnerability by not making myself a target of the group's callous attention. Because my need to minimize was the more powerful of the two intentions, my behavior followed suit; I avoided becoming the target of the group, but at a steep price: I didn't speak up.

A Universal Tendency

In sharing my playground example in workshops around the globe, I've found that minimizing—the conversational manifestation of the flight response—is a problem almost everyone can relate to. In a leadership development program at a Fortune 10 company, for instance, a senior vice president approached me to share a similar incident. "I just did the same damned thing," he said. He was in charge of one of the largest contracts in the company, and in a recent meeting with the customer, the client snapped, in a very unprofessional way, on one of this VP's junior executives. Loud, unpleasant, and harsh, the unprovoked reaction took place in front of a room of people. As the ranking executive from the company, he knew he should step in and protect his junior executive. "I knew I should do it. I could see my people looking at me to do it. It was the right thing to do. But like you on the playground, I just froze in my tracks; I just sat there and watched my guy take the abuse."

In each of these examples, conversational capacity drops because the behavior of well-intentioned people is seized by their need to play it safe. They shut down when they should speak up. They soft-pedal a point when they should assert it with force. They bring up their concerns in the hallway after a decision is made rather than in the meeting when it matters.

Minimize Behaviors

When we minimize, it's not that we don't have an agenda, it's that our agenda is subverted by a strong need to keep things comfortable, to avoid conflict, to keep things calm. When stuck between our good intentions and our need to minimize, we often slip into a variety of conversational tactics that emphasize caution at the expense of candor. What follows is a list of behaviors that we often employ when our minimizing reflex has been triggered. While far from comprehensive, the list nevertheless demonstrates the complex and varied ways the flight response manifests itself in our conversations. See if you recognize any of them:

➤ **We cover up our views, ideas, information, or concerns.** "To refrain from an act is no less an act than to commit one."[5] Like me on the playground, we don't speak up when we should.

➤ **We feign agreement or support.** We say we agree when we don't. We see this when we tell someone, "Your idea is brilliant" when we're really thinking, "I'll bet your parents are first cousins."

➤ **We engage in "hallway" dynamics.** When an issue isn't addressed in a meeting or with the person with whom we have the issue, it almost always gets aired in the hallway, the parking lot, or behind closed doors with a like-minded colleague.

➤ **We ease in.** To make an issue more palatable and less offensive, we water it down, soften it, or make it look less serious than it is. We do this when we sugarcoat our opinions, downplay our point before we make it, or butter someone up before we dump bad news on him or her.

➤ **We prematurely withdraw.** We pull the rip cord on the conversations and bail out before we make progress because our need to keep out of trouble overwhelms our desire for progress.

➤ **We gradually reveal our point.** Like someone sticking a toe in the water to test the temperature, we often employ a "strategy of gradual revelation,"[6] slowly letting our opinions or judgments trickle out into the open, in an attempt to avoid triggering a defensive reaction in others.

➤ **We ask leading questions.** Rather than make our point directly, we'll ask a series of questions designed to "lead" the other person to our point. "So, do you think that was a good way to run the meeting yesterday? Do you think you might have done a few things differently? I am just thinking out loud here, but do you think maybe an agenda would help?"

➤ **We avoid the issue or change the subject.** We steer a conversation away from any issue that might spark tension, conflict, or discomfort. When such an unwelcome issue is raised, a way to reduce the tension is to move the conversation to a safer subject.

➤ **We're deliberately ambiguous.** By speaking in foggy, obfuscated terms, we can more easily back away if someone reacts defensively.

➤ **We employ caveats.** We often pepper our language with caveats and qualifiers to make it seem less direct, offensive, or off-putting: "I'm sure this is a bad idea, but I'm wondering if perhaps we might consider the idea of maybe moving the meeting to Thursday? That's probably a bad idea, right?"

➤ **We use third-party examples.** We pretend we're talking about someone else and hope that the person we're talking with gets the message. "I know this guy, a friend of mine, who tells his people that he likes people to talk to him straight but then shoots them down when they do. I don't think he realizes he's doing it. What do you think I should tell him?" Another way we use a third party is by citing others as the source of our negative feedback or information: "I don't have a problem with your behavior. I think it's completely appropriate. But other people are really struggling with it."

➤ **We display submissive body language.** To signal that we're no threat and keep ourselves from harm's way, we limit our eye contact, lower the volume of our voices, and diminish our physical presence to make ourselves smaller targets.

➤ **We use denial.** We deny our concern for fear it will raise the tension and lead to an unpleasant consequence, saying, "No, I don't have any concerns about the strategy at all," when we really harbor grave doubts.

➤ **We make excuses.** We let people off the hook by making excuses, which reduces tension, but at the expense of learning or progress. "I am sure you have a good reason for doing what you're doing, and you're under a lot of stress, so people should just stop their whining and do what you're asking."

➤ **We take the "monkey."** Minimizers will often avoid tension or negative emotions by taking responsibility for an issue. "Don't worry about it," managers may say, "I'll take care of it," when they should let their employee deal with the problem. This self-sacrificing behavior may protect them from the short-term discomfort associated with holding others accountable, but long term it leads to the accumulation of "monkeys" —tasks that rightfully belong to others—that we've placed on our own back.[7]

➤ **We unilaterally control the situation to keep it safe and comfortable.**[8] We decide what is and isn't discussable in a conversation and then withhold from others that we are doing so. We must do this unilaterally, for if we explained that we were adopting this strategy, it would defeat the purpose of the strategy. We would never say, for instance, "I've unilaterally decided you can't handle discussing this issue without getting upset, and therefore I've decided to avoid it completely. I'm not going to tell you I am doing this because that would probably upset you, negating my strategy."

➤ **We use e-mail or voice mail to raise our concerns.** We often use voice mail or e-mail to raise our concerns, not because they're the most responsible or effective ways to express our views but because we don't have to be there for the reaction when the other person gets the message.

Think about your own experience. What other behaviors do you see yourself and others using to minimize the level of negative emotion or tension in a conversation?

Fight: When Curiosity Gives Way to Certainty

If our need to minimize—and the candor gap it produces—were the only thing constraining conversational capacity, it'd be a daunting hurdle in its own right. But, as we're about to see, we're not that lucky. There's another potent tendency that sends us flying out of the sweet spot, but in the opposite direction.

Imagine you're back in that meeting where your team is discussing a major decision about an important project, and, just as before, you have major reservations about the direction the discussion is heading. The rest of the team, including your manager, feel strongly about a particular decision, but you don't agree; you think it's the worst choice possible. You want to speak up and raise your concern even though you know it won't be popular.

But this time you experience a different intentional conflict. On one hand, you want to work with the group to make the best decision, but on the other hand, you want the others to see the error of their ways, you want them to make the *right* decision, you feel a passionate need to save them from their mistake by swaying them to your point of view.

There's a good chance you don't consciously recognize this intentional conflict either. You just *feel* the overpowering need to convince the team there's a better way to approach the problem.

Because the emotional reaction emanating from your lower brain is so strong, you go into behavioral autopilot; raising your voice, putting forward your view in forceful terms, discounting the logic of others, and arguing with anyone who dares to disagree, all in an attempt to "*win*"[9] the conversation, be right, and get your way.

The Sweet Spot

Minimize ←————— ● —————→ *Win*

When we're hijacked by our need to win, our behavior is driven by a competitive, self-serving logic: "This conversation is a zero-sum contest. Someone's going to win. Someone's going to lose. *I don't like to lose.*" Motivated by our need to be right, our mind shuts and our mouth opens, and we grow increasingly arrogant and argumentative. As our curiosity withers and our certainty expands, we push our agenda onto others because our sense of effectiveness is contingent on getting other people to see things our way and agree with us.

How powerful is this tendency? As the conversational manifestation of the *fight* response, it can trigger intense reactions that easily overwhelm our intended behavior. Take the case of two doctors who got into a heated argument over who should perform an emergency cesarean section on a 32-year-old woman. The mother wanted the doctor who had overseen her prenatal care to perform the surgery, but the duty doctor pulled rank and claimed it was his job. Their argument quickly escalated to fisticuffs even as the mother pleaded with them "stop fighting and help me."[10]

"It was a big fight," said the husband. "They ended up rolling around on the floor. And my wife was screaming for them to stop."[11]

An hour and a half after the fight was broken up, a third doctor arrived to perform the operation, but it was too late. The baby girl was stillborn.

I have no doubt both these doctors initially *intended* to help their patient, but their need to win the argument about the surgery dramatically overpowered their professional intentions. They sacrificed the health of the mother and her child because of their primal need to get their way.

When we trigger toward the win side of the behavioral spectrum, we act as if there is a moral imperative to convince people to see things our way and agree with us. "We all know what it feels like when the moralization switch flips inside us," says Steven Pinker, "the righteous glow, the burning dudgeon, and the drive to recruit others to the cause."[12]

The Human Flamethrower

This need to win is stronger in some people than it is in others. I first met the "human flamethrower" at a workshop conducted with his team—an international, cross-functional group at a large organization in the southwestern United States. I was involved because the team members were having trouble working together, a problem largely driven by the Flamethrower's combative behavior. Compelled by an unbridled need to win, he pushed his teammates out of every conversation and meeting with his over-the-top, "I'm right, you're wrong" reactions.

"At my family dinner table," the Flamethrower told me, "rabid religious and political discussion was normal. We really went at it. If you *weren't* arguing at the dinner table, Mom thought you weren't feeling well," he said. "I thought all families were like mine until I started bringing friends home for dinner," he explained. "They would leave with post-traumatic stress disorder—totally shell-shocked by the way my family talked to each other." He said that when he asked his friends why they were reacting so negatively, they would say, "All your family does is fight."

"So I would argue with them," he said, "trying to convince them that it wasn't fighting; it was just 'dinner chat.'"

After spending 18 of the most formative years of his life in that combustible family environment, the Flamethrower didn't leave behind his well-practiced need to win when he left home for school and then work. And it was his well-practiced inflammatory style that earned him his nickname in this team, where he was a win-driven arsonist in a group of minimizing tinder. "Working with him," sighed one beleaguered colleague, "is pure hell."

The Flamethrower wasn't a malicious person. Witty, engaging, and articulate, at a company dinner you wanted to be seated at his table. He was the life of the party. But it was no party when he disagreed with you in a meeting. He would pounce on any idea he didn't like and assert his own opinions with such force that it made others feel reluctant, even stupid, to challenge him. He treated his perspective as truth, the obvious standard by which other views should be judged. In a single blazing sentence, he'd advocate an idea as if its validity was patently evident, and shoot down an opposing idea as if it was the dumbest thing he'd ever heard.

Not surprisingly, his strong win behavior produced a losing dynamic. His colleagues, lacking the conversational capacity to deal with the Flamethrower's aggressive conduct, shut down, avoided discussion, feigned agreement, and generally minimized their exposure to his verbal onslaughts. When the team's performance sputtered, the Flamethrower—who genuinely wanted to be part of a high-performance team—triggered into more pugnacious behavior in an attempt to shift his colleagues into a higher gear. But of course it didn't work. The harder he pushed his team to engage, the more his colleagues retreated, and the more the team members retreated, the harder he pushed them to engage. The Flamethrower's win behavior—and his team's inability to deal with it—fueled a downward spiral of dysfunction.

It's a Formidable Tendency

When it contradicts our objectives in a conversation, our need to win produces a crippling *intentional conflict*. On the one hand we want to work with others. On the other hand, we want them to think and do things our way. The doctors in the surgery wanted to help the patient, but they also wanted to "win" the argument about how to perform the procedure. Each doctor was of two minds: "My allegiance to the Hippocratic oath is telling me to help the patient, but my win tendency is telling me to punch my colleague."

In his classic text *Teaching Thinking*, Edward De Bono sheds light on this potent reaction:

> *The need to be right at all times is a more powerful objective than most in determining the direction of thinking. A person will use his thinking to keep himself right and then believe whatever position that thinking has generated. This is especially true with more able pupils, whose egos have been built up over the years on the basis that they are brighter than the other pupils. Such a person finds it very difficult to admit a mistake and almost as difficult to acknowledge the value of someone else's idea. Thinking is no longer used as an exploration of the subject area but as an ego-support device. Thinking is used to support an initial judgment. The objectivity required in truly skillful thinking is completely lacking. Yet the arguments that result may be brilliantly logical and consistent.*"[13]

I like the dual meaning of the word "arguments" in that last sentence.

Technically Smart but Conversationally Dumb

One person with a strong win tendency can dumb down an entire team of smart people if they lack the capacity to deal with his or her behavior. I saw this demonstrated in a team at an engineering firm managing a project beset by daunting technical hurdles. But this team's biggest problem wasn't technical; it was the team members' inability to deal with Doug, the smartest engineering mind on the program and a person with a fanatical need to get his way. Doug's take-no-prisoners behavior was emboldened by his stellar academic background, his deep well of experience, his encyclopedic memory, and his sharp, analytical mind. To top it all off, he also had a quick tongue and a booming voice.

Doug used all of these factors like a bludgeon to beat others out of discussions and decisions. He dominated meetings with his shock-and-awe conversational style, which included shutting down his teammates, interrupting people who expressed views that competed with his own, and escalating the intensity of his response if a "wrong" view was gaining ground. The team was so browbeaten by Doug's fierce behavior that his mere presence killed the team's conversational capacity.

It's a Common Problem

This tendency to "win" is far more common than we appreciate, and it's not just a problem at work. M. Scott Peck describes being triggered while playing a game of chess with his teenage daughter. One night, after several weeks of pleading with her dad to play chess with her, his daughter got her wish when he asked her if she wanted to play. "She eagerly accepted and we soon settled down to a most even and challenging match," Peck explains.

"It was a school night, however, and at nine o'clock my daughter asked if I could hurry up my moves, because she needed to get to bed; she had to get up at six in the morning. I knew her to be rigidly disciplined in her sleeping habits, and it seemed that she ought to be able to give up some of this rigidity." The conversation went downhill from there. "I told her 'Come on, you can go to bed a little later for once. You shouldn't start games that you can't finish. We're having fun." He shares what happened next:

> *We played on for another fifteen minutes, during which time she became visibly discomfited. Finally, she pleaded, "Please, Daddy, please hurry your moves." "No goddamnit," I replied. "Chess is a serious game. If you're going to play it well, you're going to play it slowly. If you don't want to play it seriously, you might as well not play it at all." And so, with her feeling miserable, we continued for another ten minutes, until suddenly my daughter burst into tears, yelled that she conceded the stupid game, and ran weeping up the stairs.[14]*

He goes on to explain how his need to get his way worked against his loving intentions. "I had started the evening wanting to have a happy time with my daughter. Ninety minutes later she was in tears and so angry at me she could hardly speak. What had gone wrong?" His answer sums up the key point we've been exploring:

> *The answer was obvious. But I did not want to see the answer, so it took me two hours to wade through the pain of accepting the fact that I had botched the evening by allowing my desire to win a chess game become more important than my desire to build a relationship with my daughter. I was depressed in earnest then. How had I gotten so out of balance? Gradually it dawned on me that my desire to win was too great [emphasis mine] and . . . somehow I had to change, for I knew that my enthusiasm, my competitiveness and my seriousness were part of a behavior pattern that was working and would continue to work toward alienating my children from me, and that if I was not able to modify this pattern, there would be other times of unnecessary tears and bitterness.*

Peck's example illustrates the basic problem: when we're triggered by our need to win, we become overly attached to our view, unable to subject it to scrutiny because all our mental effort goes into selling the perspective. Any issue can set off our need to win, but especially those ideas that contradict our current ways of thinking, our notions of what is acceptable, proper, or right. When we snap into win mode, we circle our cognitive wagons and load our conversational guns, ready to defend our current map of reality from all foes. We become dogmatic and close down when we should get curious and open up.

Win Behaviors

Here is a partial list of behaviors you might see, from yourself and from others, when our intentions are hijacked by our need to be right:

> ➤ **We state our positions as fact.** We'll put forward our views in absolutistic terms, as if anyone who sees things differently is in need of remedial assistance. We say things like, "The fact of the matter is . . ." or, "If you were looking at this clearly you'd realize that . . ." or, "Anyone with any experience in this industry knows . . ."

> ➤ **We dismiss or discount alternative views and perspectives.** We'll ignore, shoot down, or make light of ideas that conflict with our own.

> ➤ **We solicit support.** We encourage people who *agree* with us to share their views. "Pam, you agree with me on this, back me up here."

> ➤ **We do little genuine listening.** We do very little genuine listening, or we listen selectively, for things we can use to bolster our point. We embody a phrase I once saw

printed on a T-shirt: "I've stopped listening. Why haven't you stopped talking?"

➤ **We don't inquire into alternative points of view.** Why waste time inquiring into an erroneous perspective, we tell ourselves, when we could be spending more productive time on our own correct one? "I'm not being difficult by refusing to explore views I know are wrong," we say to ourselves, "I'm just being efficient!"

➤ **We interrupt.** We cut people off, especially when they share a view that contradicts our own.

➤ **We display aggressive body language.** We expand our physical presence, using laser-beam eye contact, expressive gestures, and a raised voice, all in an effort to be more intimidating and persuasive.

➤ **We use dismissive body language.** Win behavior is not always highly dramatic. Sometimes a simple roll of the eyes, a heavy sigh, or a sarcastic remark is all that's needed to write off a comment or perspective.

➤ **We reject feedback or input.** Convinced we're right, and closed off to criticism or suggestion, we react to feedback as a harsh indictment of our worth or competence. "Shut up. Don't tell me what to do."

➤ **We label or demonize people who have different views.** We characterize them as misinformed, non–team players, heretics, morons, or malcontents.

➤ **We use hyperbole.** "If we don't do what I'm suggesting, this whole project is doomed."

➤ **We pontificate.** We adopt an air of superiority or expertise in order to give imaginary weight to our views.

➤ **We pull rank.** We use our authority, or our relationship to it, to overpower the ideas of others. We say things like "You can read an org chart, right? So while I appreciate your concerns we're going to do it my way." Or, "Every expert on the subject agrees with me on this."

➤ **We ask dismissive or belittling questions to put down a view we don't like.** "You're not so naive that you really think that will work, are you?" or "Did you even think about that before you suggested it?"

➤ **We unilaterally control the situation to "win."** We unilaterally decide when and how to address an issue so our idea has a better chance of "winning."

Think about your own experience. What else do you see yourself and others doing to "win" a conversation?

Often several of these behaviors are employed in combination. This is easy to see in political rhetoric, where politicians and pundits alike put forward their opinions as fact, dismiss the views of others, demonize people who don't agree with them, and show little to no interest in listening to others. They radiate the arrogant, narrow-minded attitude of, "I know what is right. I know what this country is about. I've got things figured out. I can't believe other people are so stupid." With such infantile patterns of conversation on regular display, is it any wonder we're increasingly repulsed by political discourse?

Both Directions at Once

In many meetings, when a tough issue hits the agenda, these mindless reactions pull a team in both directions at once. As the Flamethrower heats up, his colleagues shut down, their conflicting reactions pushing each other farther and farther out of the sweet spot.

The Sweet Spot

Minimize ←————————— ● —————————→ *Win*

This is especially true when one person has more authority than the others. A manager, just by walking into a meeting, can dramatically decrease the conversational capacity of her teammates because her authority triggers their need to minimize. And, if this wasn't a big enough barrier to openness, even a minor win reaction from her position of power lowers conversational capacity far more dramatically than the same behavior coming from a peer because her authority *amplifies* her behavior.

This is an important point. If we're a manager, our job is to attract the smartest and most experienced people we can, and to create a culture where they can apply their skills and knowledge to the challenges at hand. If they're not speaking up, they're being paid for something they're not providing. But the harsh reality is that our own management behavior may be *stifling* their abilities to contribute. By failing to compensate for the minimizing effect our authority has on our people, and, even more egregiously, when we trigger into win behavior, we encourage our people to minimize, guaranteeing we won't get full access to their knowledge, expertise, ideas, and suggestions. This problem has been well documented in healthcare. The *New York Times* reported that a "survey by the Institute for Safe Medication Practices, a nonprofit organization, found that 40 percent of hospital staff members reported having been so intimidated by a doctor that they did not share their concerns about orders for medication that appeared to be incorrect."[15]

We All Do Both

"Which tendency affects my behavior?" you might be wondering. But that's not the most useful question to consider. The Russian author Aleksandr Solzhenitsyn observed that the line that divides good and evil runs through the heart of every human being. The same can be said for the line between minimizing and winning. While no one is *just* a minimizer or *just* a winner, most of us do have a dominant tendency. Like the bass and treble settings on a car radio, our minimize and win tendencies are often set at different levels. The Flamethrower's win tendency was dialed up high, for example, and his minimize tendency was dialed down low; his colleague's settings were almost exactly the opposite. It's no wonder they had such a hard time working in the sweet spot.

"The unexamined life is not worth living," argued Socrates. Since we can demonstrate both tendencies in a meeting—triggering to minimize on one issue, shifting gears to win on the next—in the spirit of personal reflection and inquiry, excellent questions to consider include the following:

> ➤ Under what circumstances in life do I find myself minimizing at the expense of my effectiveness?
> ➤ Under what circumstances do I let go of curiosity and argue to win at the expense of my good intentions?

We'll all answer these questions differently. Our unique personalities, upbringing, education, and life experiences guarantee we'll all react in different ways. A situation that sends you flying into an aggressive win stance may trigger you to cave in and minimize.

Typical Triggers

"The more we need to work through others," says Harvard's Joan Magretta, "the better we need to understand ourselves."[16] If we want to be more aware of the impact these tendencies have on our behavior, it's essential we pay closer attention to how we're reacting in meetings and conversations. When we lose it and leave the sweet spot, note what happened. What was the trigger? Was it the issue? The person? The way he or she treated us? Did someone cut us off on the way to work this morning, and now we're screaming at our colleague in a meeting? It's important to become more mindful of these habitual reactions because we have no hope of managing a reaction we can't see. And, because almost every conversation provides a valuable chance to learn, we can use our day-to-day work experience to observe and reflect, increasing our awareness of our tendencies and subtle (and not so subtle) ways they throw us off our games.

To help you with this process of reflection and observation, here is a list of common triggers that send us out of the sweet spot, one way or the other:

> **How much we care about the issue.** The more we care, the more likely we are to be triggered.

> **Our formal position in the hierarchy.** Our place in the pecking order is a big factor. Given our natural deference to authority, in a dominance hierarchy we generally minimize up the chain of command and win down it.

> **Status.** What is my standing in the group? Am I new, or am I an established member of the team? Am I highly respected or routinely ignored?

> **Expertise.** When we feel like we know more about the subject than our teammates, we may be more inclined to

win behavior. But when we feel we know less than our colleagues, we're often more inclined to cover up our views and minimize—even if we have a useful idea.

➤ **The behavior of others.** Our behavior is often a knee-jerk reaction to the behavior of others. The win reaction of someone in a meeting, for instance, can trigger me to minimize, and at the same time, trigger another colleague to win. If we're that manipulatable, we'd have to admit, "I can easily balance candor and curiosity when other people let me."

➤ **Personality.** An introvert, for instance, may be more inclined to minimize during a meeting, while his extroverted colleague may be far more likely to argue.

➤ **Culture.** Our family, national, ethnic, corporate, or functional culture can be a big influence over when and how we lose balance.

➤ **The perceived risk of speaking up.** If we perceive the risk of speaking up to be high, we may lose candor and minimize.

➤ **The perceived risk of not speaking up.** If we perceive the risk of not speaking up to be high, we may lose curiosity and argue our point.

A wide range of factors can trigger our need to minimize or win. What else would you add to the list?

Learning to recognize our tendencies and triggers provides us with two distinct advantages. First, as we've already covered, we can't manage something we can't see, so only by developing the capacity to recognize when we're leaving the sweet spot do we have any hope of staying in it.

Second, awareness of these tendencies, and how easily they throw us off our intentions, generates more empathy, a more compassionate view of people who behave in ways that we don't understand. Aware of how easily our own intentions are hijacked, we're more likely to consider that others may have decent intentions that are being overrun by their need to minimize or win. This empathetic mindset makes us less critical and more curious when others behave in ways that strike us as odd. We're more likely to think, "I wonder what's going on here?" or "I wonder why he's reacting this way?" as opposed to, "What an ass."

Are Minimize and Win Behaviors Always Bad?

Given all the mischief they cause, it's tempting to pathologize our primal tendencies and treat them as unadulterated evils. But that would be unwise, for there are times when these tendencies actually serve our good intentions. If I'm at dinner with a client and he brings up a political perspective that runs counter to mine, what's the smart thing to do? Unless my goals for the evening include arguing with my client over politics, minimizing makes perfect sense. On the other hand, my younger brother is a paramedic-firefighter in Alameda County, California, and when he shows up at the scene of an accident and a life is at stake, he kicks into aggressive win behavior to mobilize people and resources to save the victim's life. It's competent behavior in that context. So it's not the behaviors themselves we should be concerned about, but the alignment between our behaviors and our intentions, and the fight-or-flight reactions that so easily pull them apart.

Moving Beyond Awareness

Now that we've reached the end of this chapter, I'm hoping you'll never experience a meeting or conversation the same way again. Armed with a new set of distinctions you'll pay more rigorous attention to your own behavior, and to the behavior of others, clearly recognizing the telltale symptoms when conversational capacity is low.

But awareness is not the same as skill. A drowning man may know he's drowning, but his awareness is no substitute for the ability to swim. So in the next chapter we'll move beyond awareness and begin exploring a proven discipline—a conversational martial art—that enables us to balance candor and curiosity in even the toughest of circumstances.

Beyond Fight and Flight

A MORE INTENTIONAL MINDSET

....

Our view of reality is like a map with which
to negotiate the terrain of life.
If the map is true and accurate, we will generally
know where we are, and if we have decided
where we want to go, we will generally know
how to get there.
If the map is false and inaccurate,
we generally will be lost.

M. SCOTT PECK

C learly our win and minimize predilections aren't the best
navigational beacons if we're seeking balanced dialogue under pressure, so we need a new map and compass if we're
to chart a more deliberate behavioral path. To that end, in this chapter we'll explore a new way of thinking that intentionally subordi-
nates our fight-or-flight reactions to a loftier set of goals. To ensure
this new way of thinking is more than just a hollow set of ideas, in
the next chapter I'll introduce skills for putting it into daily practice.
This combination is essential, for a mindset without actionable skills

is impotent, and skills without a guiding framework are aimless.

This new way of thinking and acting represents a tectonic shift in how we approach tough conversations. Together they create a practical *discipline* that builds conversational capacity, enabling a team to perform effectively in the most challenging of circumstances.

Before we dive in, there are three things to emphasize. First, this discipline is not simply the *opposite* of our habituated tendencies. We're not going to increase our conversational capacity by *maximizing* negative emotions and *losing* conversations. Second, this discipline doesn't *replace* our natural fight-or-flight reactions; they're hard-wired, and no amount of skill is going to eradicate these instinctual drives. Our only option is to better recognize and manage them, which takes us to the last point: This discipline is not a simple *gimmick*, something we can easily master with minimal effort and practice. It's a conversational martial art, and earning our black belt—the ability to remain balanced in the toughest of circumstances—takes dedicated focus and practice.

Einstein observed that it's impossible to solve problems with the same thinking we used to create them. To rise above our hereditary predispositions and bolster our conversational capacity, therefore, we need a new way of thinking—a guiding *mindset*—that encourages us to balance candor and curiosity.

A Cognitive Shift

This mindset reframes what it means to be effective when we converse with people about important issues by setting aside our primal tendencies for a higher set of objectives. This is not a casual undertaking. It requires sacrifice. If we have a strong minimize tendency, for example, we'll have to abandon our need to be safe and comfortable if we want to be more effective. The Flamethrower, by contrast, had to forfeit his need to be right all the time to reach the levels of performance he expected of his team.

This is easier said than done. It requires tremendous energy to break free of the gravitational pull of our programmed responses and establish a new behavioral trajectory. We never fully appreciate the tight hold our minimize and win tendencies have on our behavior until, in the heat of the moment, we try to behave in a way that directly contradicts them.

To establish this new trajectory we adopt a new focal point—a goal worth the energy we're expending to achieve it. Our attention centers on four interrelated objectives:

➤ Making informed and effective choices

➤ Expanding our awareness by leaning into different views

➤ Generating internal commitment to the choices we make

➤ Establishing joint control

Informed and Effective Choice

The hallmark objective in this new way of thinking is *informed and effective choice*.[1] If we're to stay firmly grounded in the sweet spot, we need to be genuinely more interested in making informed decisions than in being comfortable or being right. But while the pursuit of informed decisions seems obvious, it's not something we naturally do. Our brain, it turns out, doesn't prefer an informed view of reality; it prefers instead a biased, self-serving view that reinforces our current perspective, reassuring us that our way of seeing the world is right and true.

In her engaging book *A Mind of Its Own*, psychologist Cordelia Fine writes about the plethora of ways our mind *avoids* being fully informed. "We find research convincing and sound if the results happen to confirm our point of view. However, we will find the exact same research method shoddy and flawed if the results fail to agree with our opinions."[2] We use our opinions to evaluate research, in other words, instead of using research to evaluate our opinions—an inclination that fortifies our current mental maps of reality. "By calling on powerful biases in memory and reasoning," Fine says, we "selectively edit and censor the truth, both about ourselves and the world, making for a softer, kinder, and altogether more palatable reality.[3] She knows this is not comforting news:

> *Being confronted with the evidence of the distorting and deceptive window dressings of the brain is unsettling, and rightly so. A brain with a mind of its own belies our strong sense that the world is just as it seems to us, and our misguided belief that our vision of "out there" is sharp and true. In fact, it appears that our attitudes are the muddled outcome of many struggling factors. Tussling against our desire to know the truth about the world are powerful drives to protect our self-esteem, sense of security, and pre-existing point of view. Set against our undeniably impressive powers of cognition are a multitude of irrationalities, biases, and quirks that surreptitiously undermine the accuracy of our beliefs.[4]*

Given our brain's fervent predilection for ego-friendly ideas and information, when we make a decision based solely on our own perspective, it's not an *informed* choice—it's a *biased* one. Our functional, educational, cultural, and experiential filters lead us to see the world in narrow, prescribed ways, and the inevitable blind spots in these views lead to choices that are more slanted and self-serving than richly informed.

So the pivotal question we have to ask ourselves is this: do we want to participate in conversations in a way that leads to informed choice, or willful ignorance? If we continue to let our minimize and win tendencies dictate our behavior, we're making a choice for the latter. But if we're interested in being more effective under stress—better able to align our intentions and our actions—we'll rein in the baser aspects of our humanity, clearly focused on making the most informed and effective choices possible.

Expanded Awareness

In our quest to make informed choices, there's no substitute for actually *being* informed. So when we place a premium on thoughtful decisions, we seek out, prefer, and lean into people with different views, information, and ideas—not because we enjoy being uncomfortable or wrong, but because we know that if we want to expand our thinking, *it's the people who see things differently that provide the most value.* "I have a view of 'reality' in my head," we basically say to others, "and you have a view of 'reality' in yours. Let's put them together to see what we can learn about this choice we're facing." We seek out and explore contrasting viewpoints, knowing the more robust, multifaceted, and vetted our view of a problem, the wiser the choices we're in a position to make.

It's like preparing for an international trip. If I realized that a business trip affords me a free day in Barcelona, I'd immediately begin exploring ways to spend my time. I'd research travel sites online to see what options were available, I'd read books, talk to friends and colleagues about what I ought to see and do, and look into hiring a personal guide to show me around the city. In short, I'd pool as much information as possible to make informed choices about how to best spend my day. In the pursuit of making the best decisions, I'd be more interested in people with ideas and experiences that *contrasted* with mine, recognizing that they're the people who will help expand my options to include things I'd never otherwise consider.

It's no different in business. When we're making an acquisition, initiating a major change process, or wrestling with a tough decision, we want access to as much information and as many perspectives as possible to expand our options for effectively tackling the challenge. We want to reduce the number of blind spots in our view of the situation we're facing.

But while this approach is easy when the issue is simple, under pressure we tend to drop this curious, open-minded drive to expand our thinking and tenaciously stick with what we "know." Pooling perspectives forces conflicts, disagreements, and ambiguities into the open, easily triggering our minimize tendencies. The conformity seen in corporate boardrooms offers an example. Given their enormous responsibilities, a board should be an open forum for a wide variety of ideas, information, opinions, and perspectives. To ensure the best decisions are made, divergent viewpoints should be vigorously shared and explored. But in far too many boards, as Jeffrey Sonnenfeld showed, this does not happen. When things get tough, board members routinely minimize—avoiding their differences, feigning agreement, or talking in the hallway.

But it's not just our minimize tendency that gets in the way. Pooling perspectives can just as easily trigger our *win* tendency, leading our behavior to work directly against informed choice. We saw this in the last chapter when two doctors disagreed about *who* would perform a C-section. Rather than explore their conflicting perspectives in search of the best decision, they slugged it out, leaving the helpless mother and her unborn daughter to suffer on the table.

When we rise above these tendencies and lean into difference, we're not seeking agreement per se, but to expand or improve our view of "reality," knowing that a major "aha" moment isn't going to come from someone who sees things the way we do—it's likely to come from someone with a contrasting perspective. "We meet aliens every day who have something to give us," says William Shatner. "They come in the form of people with different opinions."[5] If we have a marketing background, the "alien" across the table with years of sales experience is more likely to help us find a weak spot in our thinking than the like-minded colleague on our marketing team. When we're truly dedicated to expanding our thinking and making informed choices, difference is our greatest ally. "Without conflicting frames of reference," says Ron Heifetz, "the social system scrutinizes only limited features of its problematic environment. It operates at the mercy of its blind spots because it cannot prepare for what it does not see."[6] If we want to move beyond our "insular prejudices"[7] and detect and correct any deficiencies in our mental maps of reality, we must approach conversations with an attitude of "You help me find my blind spots and I'll help you find yours."

Lincoln

In a fortuitous mix of man, mindset, and mess, Abraham Lincoln provides a remarkable example of this thought process in action. Upon his election, he faced a monumental challenge—an impending Civil War and the calamitous failure of the American experiment. To deal with this leadership challenge, Lincoln did something unusual in American politics—he pulled into his cabinet his political *enemies*. Demonstrating a unique way of thinking about how to build a useful team, he pulled into his cabinet a group of men with ideas that dramatically conflicted not only with his views, but with those of each other as well. Rather than assemble a cabinet of like-minded colleagues to help him advance his political agenda, he opted instead for a team of rivals. Doris Kearns-Goodwin, author of the renowned book *Team of Rivals*,[8] says, "Every major stream of American political thought was represented in the Lincoln cabinet."[9] It was a hornet's nest of competing political perspectives.

Lincoln didn't assemble this cabinet of contradiction because he was a minimizer and enjoyed calm and comfortable meetings. And he certainly didn't do it because he liked to "win" every conversation and be right. Lincoln did it because the eclectic viewpoints in this cabinet allowed him to make far more sophisticated, nuanced, and informed decisions about how to deal with the complicated realities facing the country. He epitomized this prescient observation made by Peter Elbow: "The surest way to get hold of what your present frame binds you to is to adopt the opposite frame. A person who can live with contradiction and exploit it—who can use conflicting models—can simply see and think more."[10]

The example set by Lincoln is instructive. The more diverse the information and perspectives to which we have access, the wiser, more informed choices we're able to make about tough, complex issues because we're able to see and think more.

Internal Commitment

There's yet another benefit to pulling the ideas and perspectives of others into the decision-making process—it fosters a higher sense of ownership for the decisions we do make. Why does this matter? Because our level of internal commitment directly correlates with how much energy we put into enacting the decision. It's important to get this right. It makes no sense to put a lot of effort into making an informed decision that no one will lift a finger to implement.

Corn Nuts

No matter our role, we yearn to feel we're more than just passive pawns in the process, that we're being listened to, that our ideas are being taken into account. We want to feel internal commitment[11] to the decisions that affect us, and we feel more connected to, and more buy-in for, those decisions that we understand and help make. This makes all the difference when it comes to implementation. High internal commitment increases the likelihood that people will roll up their sleeves to help implement a decision. Low internal commitment, by contrast, has the opposite effect; it increases the odds that people will sit idle, doing as little as possible to move the decision forward. Even more worrisome, it increases the risk that they'll actually roll up their sleeves and *block* implementation.

I know this from direct experience. As a young kid, I was forced to wear braces. As a result of having that decision made *for* me, against my will and without my input, my internal commitment to the braces was exceptionally low. This created a major problem because, for braces to work, the orthodontist needs the willing cooperation of the person wearing them. My orthodontist didn't have that from me. My low commitment had exactly the opposite effect—it provoked an antagonistic, passive-aggressive response. Passively, I refused to wear my rubber bands or my headgear. Aggressively, I ate everything I was told to avoid. Hanging on the fridge, for example, was a list of foods I was supposed to shun. I treated it like a checklist: Apples. *Check.* Popcorn. *Check.* Hard candy. *Check.* In the process I got addicted to large fried kernels of savory corn that are hard as rocks. If you're eager to sabotage your braces, it's hard to find a better snack food.

The consequence of my ill-advised behavior was predictable. After 18 months of escalating frustration between my parents, the orthodontist, and myself, I had the braces taken off prematurely. I wasted heaps of time and money, strained my relationship with my parents, and my teeth are still crooked—but at least I "won."

I often suggest to managers and executives that their people are doing to their organizations' strategies, change processes, or decisions the same thing I did to my braces. When important decisions are just handed down to them like a gift (with good intentions—much like my parents and the braces) the internal commitment to the process is often low, and sometimes nonexistent. Lacking input, counsel, explanation, and involvement—things that tend to produce greater understanding and a higher sense of ownership—we feel less like a responsible, engaged partner helping drive implementation and more like a passive passenger on a bus—not exactly a prescription for a lot of buy-in. This lack of commitment costs us dearly. At best we get lackluster implementation; at worst, we get corn nuts.

Contrast my orthodontic fiasco with the experience of my youngest son, Carl. With orthodontic problems even more severe than mine, my wife Renee and I knew he needed braces. But we decided on a very different approach to the decision. Carl reacted negatively when we first broached the subject of braces, a reaction I understood all too well. "We're not going to force you to get braces," I told him. "That happened to me, and it won't happen to you. I'm not paying thousands of dollars just to get you addicted to CornNuts."

We decided on a process that would allow Carl to make an informed decision about whether or not he wanted braces. As his parents, we suggested he should get them for aesthetic and social reasons—he was starting high school soon and straight teeth would be a plus. We also took him to an orthodontist who provided a more technical perspective. The orthodontist explained the problems Carl faced, the treatment options available, and, perhaps most important, he explained the problems Carl would confront later in life if he chose *not* to get his teeth fixed now. That was sobering information.

We then gave Carl a week to think about it. At the end of the week we asked Carl what he wanted to do. "I want braces," he said, matter-of-factly. It wasn't a fun or easy decision. He wasn't jumping up and down about it. But it was an *informed* decision, and it was *his* decision. In dramatic contrast with my experience, Carl was a model of internal commitment, always reminding us about appointments, wearing the appropriate gear, and avoiding the right foods. His braces are off now and he has a brilliant smile.

When we're dedicated to informed and effective choices, we pull people into decision-making or problem-solving processes because they're useful in two ways. First, involving key players leads to better information and more robust decisions because we have access to their thinking. Second, those same people feel more connected to the decisions that do get made. It's a double win; we get better decisions that are more effectively implemented.

Commitment isn't dependent on agreement. We can internally commit to something we don't fully agree with, but only if we understand it and feel our thinking has been taken into account, that it's had an impact—even if it's just to highlight a risk or an alternative option. We need to respect the *process* by which the decision was made, not fully concur with the decision itself. "I don't agree with the decision," a team member might say, "but understand it, and I like the way our manager made it." When the process is fair, transparent, and balanced, and we've played an active role, we tend to feel more buy-in to the output.

Joint Control

When we need to work with other people to solve a problem or make a decision, we only have two options for how to go about it: guess what will work and impose it on the people we're working with, or involve them and have them jointly control *what* we're trying to achieve and *how* we're working to achieve it. When we guess, we *unilaterally* make choices based on our assumptions of what will work, of what others expect of us, and of how they're likely to react or behave in the process.[12] Put differently, we impose on others *our* view of the best way to deal with the situation at hand, deciding how to both define and solve the problem in our own little private intellectual Idaho. It's unilateral—we involve no one else in the process.

This is easy to see in management. All too often managers unilaterally define what it means to be an effective manager, and then impose their definitions on their people, wondering later why their 360-degree feedback never improves. I saw this in an executive with a strong minimize tendency who unilaterally dealt with performance problems in his team by sending his staff articles related to their developmental needs. He sent the articles via interoffice mail accompanied by a short, handwritten note: "I thought you might like this," or, "This author had some good ideas." He never explained that the articles were his way of providing feedback.

When I asked why he didn't just sit down with them and share his concerns directly, he said, "That makes me uncomfortable. I've never been good with conflict." He unilaterally assumed that providing the feedback directly would provoke an unpleasant experience, and then he unilaterally covered up that he was angling for a behavior change when he sent articles to do his work for him. I asked him if people correctly interpreted the articles as a hint that they needed to improve in some area. "Sometimes they do," he replied.

"So what do you do when people don't get it?" I asked.

"I send more articles."

Unilateral control leads to uninformed decisions and lower internal commitment because we're only using our biased brain to decide how to work effectively with others. But failing to involve others in these decisions is a recipe for incompetence. Rather than take their ideas into account so we can make a more informed and effective choice, we opt instead for an uninformed, cross-our-fingers choice.

Customer service provides another common example. All too often we unilaterally define good customer service and impose it on our customers, and then wonder why our customer service scores never improve. And, when this happens, who are we likely to blame? The customer, of course. The source of the failure, however, is not the customer, but the unilateral interpretation of good customer service we're imposing on them. It's as if we say to our customers, "We want to provide exceptional customer service, but we have our own idea of what good customer service entails, and we're going to unilaterally impose it on you. If you don't appreciate the customer service we unilaterally provide you, we'll roll our eyes, blame you, and label you 'difficult,' or 'high maintenance.'"

Contrast this unilateral approach with the more learning-focused joint control, where we proactively make our goals and concerns explicit and ask others to help us manage them. This is a far more effective way to make informed and effective decisions because we're involving others in the important decisions for how to best achieve the desired objectives. We exercise joint control by inquiring into the ideas of others about such things as effective customer service, management, or meetings in order to make wiser choices about how to design and implement our actions.

We can see what this looks like in practice at a large financial institution going through a major reorganization. Managers around the enterprise jointly involved their teams in the process of managing the difficult change. Rather than simply handing down their decisions from on high, or sending them articles via interoffice mail, they worked with their teams to collaboratively design the framework needed to move forward efficiently and effectively. "I want to be an effective manager as we move into this change process," they said to their teams. "My goal is to create a context where you can bring the best you have to offer to the change process we're moving into. But while I have ideas about what that might look like, I don't want to force my approach on you. I'd rather share my ideas with you and then hear yours—particularly if you have different ideas about how we can make this work."

Managers not only sought input on the change process itself, but also on how to monitor their ability to stick with their agreements. "Once we've agreed on an approach, let's jointly decide how we'll address any breakdowns that occur. If I don't behave according to our agreements, for instance, I want you to be able to raise your hand and call me on it. And, by the same token, if you're not performing to expectations, I want to make that discussable. Let's come up with a clear-cut process by which we can self-correct as a team."

This joint approach to managing a difficult change process makes the goals explicit and enrolls people in helping make choices for how best to achieve them. This not only helps managers make more intelligent choices, it shows tremendous respect for their teams and increases the buy-in their people feel to both the manager and to the process. The result? Higher commitment. Fewer corn nuts.

Whether you're a project manager, a team member, or a CEO, this is a useful way of approaching any situation where you need to work with others to be effective. Want to be a better leader? Need to improve the working relationship between people, teams, functions, or projects? Need to make changes in the most effective way possible? Want to make meetings more productive? Want to provide better customer service? There are only two options for making the necessary decisions: *guess* and hope for the best, or *ask* and pull the ideas and expectations of others into the process. By providing us access to more than just our own head to solve problems and make decisions, joint control leads to more informed and effective choices.

A customer service executive from a logistics company explained how the service team members' unilateral approach to customer service got them in trouble, and how involving their customer got them out of it. "We design our customer service using *our* metrics, but our most important customer measures it with their own," he said. "The problem is that we only recently realized that they're different metrics. This caused a lot of friction. When we provided good customer service as *our* metrics defined it, the customer is unhappy. But when they told us our service wasn't that good, we said, 'What? Sure it is. And we have the data to prove it.'"

They fundamentally changed their approach by directly involving their customers in how to define and implement their working relationship: "Our goal is to provide exceptional customer service. But we also realize that our view of customer service may differ from yours. So, if you don't mind, let us share what we think exceptional customer service looks like, as well as the metrics we use to track it, and then we'd love to get feedback from you, especially if you have different views or use different metrics. We want to make sure we're meeting *your* customer service expectations, not just ours." By adopting this shared approach, they're saying, in essence, "Help us make more informed and effective choices about the customer service we're providing you."

It May Seem Obvious

Placing our primary emphasis on making informed and effective choices may seem obvious, but as we've seen, it's not how we typically operate. Because it requires that we open up to the perspectives of people with differing and even conflicting perspectives, it can make us wrong, or uncomfortable, or both, and easily trigger our minimize and win reactions. The managers who asked, "What do you need more or less of from me so I can help you do your job more effectively?" were in positions to make better choices about how to manage their people, but the conversations that helped them make those choices weren't always an ego massage.

The main point is this: If we're going to jointly design a work relationship—between people, within teams, between teams, or between organizations—we need the capacity to untether our behavior from our habitual, self-serving, ego-driven reactions. When it comes to making informed and effective choices, our egos are the enemies of effectiveness.

Being candid and curious are two states of mind that don't easily coexist under stress. That balanced demeanor is hard to hold, and the more stressful and challenging the situation we're in, the harder it is to hold it. Focusing on informed and effective choice provides a compass to keep us headed in the right direction when our fight-or-flight reactions threaten to pull us off course. But this mindset by itself won't help us stay in the sweet spot unless we can put it to use. With that in mind, in the next chapter we'll explore specific conversational skills that move this mindset out of our head and into conversations and meetings.

Intentional Dialogue

SKILLS FOR BALANCING CANDOR AND CURIOSITY

....

Learning is not simply having a new insight
or a new idea. Learning occurs when we take effective
action, when we detect and correct error.
How do you know that you know something?
When you can produce what it is you claim to know.

CHRIS ARGYRIS

The new mindset we explored in the last chapter represents a dramatic shift in our *intentions* in a conversation. But as my playground experience illustrates, we often have clear intentions that our actions fail to match. So how is this new way of thinking to be any different? How do we align this new frame of mind and our actual behavior? In this chapter I'll answer these questions by laying out a set of skills for putting this mindset to use.

The Discipline

To start, imagine you're once again in that meeting where your team is discussing a significant problem. The rest of the team members, including your manager, favor one decision, but you strongly disagree. With much at stake, you feel compelled to speak up and raise your concern, but you again feel the powerful tug of your intentional conflicts threatening to pull you off balance. Part of you wants to play it safe and avoid being seen as a troublemaker; part of you wants to argue to keep the team from making a horrible mistake.

But this time, rather than cave in to these impulsive reactions, you remain balanced and respond in a more intentional, disciplined way. You do this by clearly putting forward your concern, explaining the reasoning behind it, and then, wary of your blind spots, you check with others to explore what you may be missing. (Perhaps you're misunderstanding what the team is considering, for instance, or maybe you're unaware of information that might change your perspective.) When a colleague responds by downplaying your concern, rather than get defensive, you ask her questions to better understand how she's seeing the issue. Despite the weight of the decision and your intentional conflicts, you're a model of collaborative learning, simultaneously candid and curious.

This is what a difficult conversation in the sweet spot looks like. "We're working hard to candidly express how *we* see things, but we're working just as hard to curiously explore how *others* are looking at the same issue. We're neither arguing nor shutting down because we're less concerned about being right or comfortable and more focused on what counts: working with our team to generate a better understanding of the issue at hand so we can make the best choice possible."

While it appears deceptively simple, responding this way requires the mindful use of four distinct skills that are extremely difficult to balance under pressure:

➤ Stating our clear *position*

➤ Explaining the underlying *thinking* that informs our position

➤ *Testing* our perspective

➤ *Inquiring* into the perspectives of others

If the mindset is what we're *thinking* in a disciplined conversation, these four behaviors are what we're *doing*.[1] The first two skills bring structure to our candor; the second two balance it with curiosity. Combined, they produce a user-friendly framework for crafting conversations that are simultaneously candid and curious.

Airto Moreira, a Brazilian jazz percussionist, was once asked how he performed improvisational jazz. "I listen to what's being played," he said, "and then I play what's missing."[2] In a similar way, this simple framework helps us see what's being "played" in a conversation, and provides skills for "playing what's missing"—allowing us to bring more balance, openness, and rigor to an otherwise defensively dysfunctional discussion.

The Sweet Spot

"Minimizing" (Low Candor) ←—— ● ——→ *(Low Curiosity) "Winning"*

or

Position and Thinking (Candor) ——→ ● ←—— *(Curiosity) Testing and Inquiry*

As we'll see, these four simple skills are a challenge to use because they pit us against our deep-seated minimize and win tendencies. Leaning into contrasting perspectives to expand our thinking may seem like a good idea, for instance, but for someone hooked on being right, it can spark a fierce, emotionally charged reaction. For a minimizer addicted to avoiding conflict, on the other hand, surfacing and exploring conflicting views, or sharing a point that contradicts the views of others, can provoke an equally debilitating emotional response. But by building our capacity to use these four skills in a balanced way, we can learn to remain focused on informed and effective choices even when our fight-or-flight reactions are doing their best to knock us off center.

That's why I refer to it as a *discipline*. That's exactly what it takes to master our habitual tendencies and remain centered and learning focused in tough situations and conversations. When our conversational capacity is high, we can maintain mindful discipline even under intense pressure. When our capacity is too low, we lose discipline and mindlessly succumb to our old, familiar, incompetent reactions under stress. Because the capacity to maintain balance under pressure is such a pivotal competence, let's look at these four skills one at a time and explore the contribution each one makes to a healthy conversation.

Candor Skill 1: We State Our Clear Position

If you're participating in a meeting with people who are putting this mindset into practice, one of the first things you'll notice is that the conversations are bold, frank, and right to the point. The skill that gives the meeting this no-nonsense, straight-spoken character comes from the first skill: the ability to state a direct, succinct *position*.

Like a topic sentence in good paragraph construction, a position statement is clear, candid, and concise. It lets others know where we stand on an issue, the specific point we're putting forward. Whether it's a view, idea, concern, or suggestion, a position should distill the essence of our view into one sentence, or no more than two. If you're back in that meeting harboring deep reservations about the direction your team is headed, you might state your position by saying, "I think the decision the team currently favors will cause more problems than it solves."

An effective position anchors the conversation with a well-defined point so that others are less likely to misunderstand the idea we're trying to communicate. Without that clarity, we increase the likelihood we'll be misinterpreted because—unless we're conversing with mind readers—we force others to make assumptions about the point we're trying to make. This is risky for two reasons: first, they often guess *incorrectly* (they're guessing with their brain, after all, not ours); and second, they tend to assume *negatively* (rather than make neutral or positive assumptions about the thoughts and motivations of others, we're inclined to assume the worst). When we fail to put forward our clear position, we open the door to needless misunderstanding and mischief because our lack of clarity muddles the dialogue.

In the John Hughes comedy *Planes, Trains, and Automobiles*, Neal Page (played by Steve Martin) lambasts the loquacious Del Griffith (played by the late John Candy), sarcastically suggesting that Del acquire this very skill: "By the way, when you're telling these little stories, here's a good idea, have a *point* [italics mine]; it makes it so much more interesting for the listener."[3]

This sage advice holds true for all of us. When we wish to put forward our view, it's a good idea to have a clear position. It's so much more helpful for the listener. Concision is key. Our point doesn't have to be perfect or detailed because it's merely a starting point, a positional pad from which we launch an unfolding discussion about the issue we're working with others to address.

For someone with a well-exercised win tendency, this skill may seem obvious and easy. The Flamethrower certainly thought so. But, for his teammates, the challenge this skill presents was daunting, especially when stating a well-defined position put them at odds with *him*. In situations that trigger our need to minimize, candor in the form of a clear position is usually the first thing to suffer.

UNCLEAR POSITION	CLEAR POSITION
• I'm wondering if we should think about doing X.	• I think we should do X.
• Do you think we might consider doing some things to make our meetings more effective?	• An agenda would dramatically improve our weekly meetings.
• "Um, you gonna stay up here as long as you can?"	• Pull up now and go around for another approach. You're going to miss the runway.
• I wonder if there's a better way to do this?	• I think there's a better way to do this.
• I kinda think that maybe option B is the best way to go, but I'm not sure.	• Option B is the best decision.

Stating our position sounds simple enough, but in my consulting work I see many people struggle to plainly state their views in one to two crisp sentences. The difficulty lies in boiling our thoughts down to their essence, forcing us to be more rigorous with how we're participating in a conversation by asking ourselves "What is it I am really trying to say? What is my *point*?"

Candor Skill 2: We Explain Our Thinking

Stating our position is a start, but to get our perspective out of our head, through our mouth, and into a conversation requires another skill on the candor side of the scale. Having stated our position, we next do our best to describe the underlying *thinking* that informs it. Rather than force others to guess how we've arrived at our point of view, we paint a verbal picture to illustrate how we came to it. When we put forward our position, we're saying, in essence, "Here is *what* I think." When we explain the thought process behind it, we're saying, "Here is *why* I think it."

Data and Interpretation

Effectively moving a view out of our brain and into a conversation requires that we articulate two things: The *data* we're paying attention to, and how we're *interpreting* that data.

A sign hanging in the Mission Evaluation Room at NASA's Johnson Space Center in Houston reads, "In God we trust, all others bring data." When, like NASA, we "bring data," there are three kinds to consider. The first kind is directly observable data—things an anthropologist could document if she were watching from the sidelines: what someone says, how they say it, his or her tone of voice and body language, as well as the visible reactions of others, and so on. It's directly observable. The second kind of data is anecdotal—a story from a newspaper article, an experience we've had in a previous situation, or an example from a book we've read. The third kind consists of measurable data—things we can track, quantify, and evaluate. This includes reports, analyses, performance metrics, financial statistics, engineering schematics, and other forms of rigorous data. By sharing the data that informs our position, we're providing a window into the logic behind our view of the problem.

But data aren't enough. To get our perspective into a conversation clearly and effectively, we must also share how we're *interpreting* the data—the logical inferences we're using to make sense of them. "Here is what I interpret these data to *mean*," we're saying, "and why I think it *matters*." Describing our interpretation of the data is essential to sharing our perspective effectively, for an engineer and a lawyer, looking at the same data, can arrive at very different ideas about their relevance. The intellectual frameworks they're each using to make sense of the data are poles apart. And it's not just our functional differences that lead us to see the world so differently. Any two people, looking at the same data, can arrive at very different conclusions about their relevance because their varying filters—educational, personality, cultural, experiential, etc.—lead them to *interpret* the data in unique ways. (We'll look into this phenomenon in greater detail in Chapter 6).

So just like a scientist putting forward a hypothesis, laying out our data and our interpretation are essential to getting our mental maps of reality into a conversation. If we provide our data without interpretation, we leave people unclear about what we think the data are telling us. If we share our interpretation but provide no data, our view seems like nothing more than a vacuous opinion.

They're Separate Skills

Putting forward a position and explaining the thinking behind it are distinct skills, and in my work I see many people who are proficient at one but have trouble with the other. Some people can effortlessly articulate their thinking on an issue, but when asked to collapse it into a clear point, they have a hard time doing it. Others suffer with the opposite problem. They're able to clearly make their point, but they struggle to describe the underlying reasons they hold it. Unless we develop the capacity to do both proficiently, we're going to be misunderstood by others—sometimes significantly. Cartha Deloach, a former assistant to J. Edgar Hoover, recalls an incident that aptly describes how easily this happens:

> *One day a memo on internal security that had been sent up to Hoover came back with a message in the familiar scrawl: "Watch the borders! H." [Emphasis mine.] Telephones began to ring all over the building, everyone asking the same question: "Is there anything going on in Mexico or Canada we should know about?" "Maybe we ought to call the Immigration and Naturalization Service." Somebody said, "Why don't you just*

ask Hoover what he knows that we don't know?" But no one wanted to show his ignorance. So we called Customs and they didn't know any more than we did. Several days later a supervisor was again reviewing the memo when the answer to the question jumped out and smacked him in the face. The memo had been typed with the narrowest possible margins. Hoover, always fastidious, had picked up his pen and in annoyance had scrawled, "Watch the borders!"[4]

"Watch the borders" is an ambiguous position (what "borders" is he referring to?), which is compounded by the lack of any explanatory thinking. Lacking that clarity, people are forced to guess what Hoover means. Not surprisingly, his people not only guessed incorrectly, they also failed to catch their error because their minimize tendencies kept them from asking Hoover to clarify his point.

These first two skills—stating a clear position and explaining the thinking that informs it—are the antidote for our tendency to minimize. They help us get our ideas, views, and perspectives into a conversation as clearly and candidly as possible. This is important. When we're in the sweet spot, we're not a passive sponge merely soaking up the perspectives of others. We have a unique viewpoint and we're working hard to get it into the pool of ideas being used to make decisions and solve problems.

It's not a popularity contest, and all views are not equal. The more rigorous, logical, and thoughtful the view, the more weight it carries. And the more expert the source, the more credence we should give the perspective. My views on conversational capacity should carry more weight than the view of someone who's never thought about the subject, just as a neurosurgeon's take on the best way to remove a brain tumor should carry infinitely more weight than mine.

Unlike a debate, it's not necessary to have our thinking flaw-lessly arranged and articulated in order to engage with others. The curiosity skills described next will help us expand, improve, and clarify our thinking to a degree unattainable on our own. That's the purpose of working in the sweet spot—to create a richer picture of the issues we're facing so we can make better choices.

By themselves, however, these candor skills aren't sufficient to reach our goal of expanding our awareness and making informed decisions. To prevent the conversation from becoming a zero-sum argument, we employ two counterbalancing skills that temper our candor with curiosity. With these two skills, we reverse the polarity in the dialogue by inviting the views of others into the conversa-tion with the same rigor and discipline with which we're putting our own view forward.

Curiosity Skill 1: We Test Our View

The first skill on the curiosity side of the scale counters our brain's natural tendency to interpret things the way it wants—in ego-sat-isfying, reality-distorting, egregiously self-serving ways. It's also an unusual skill. We weren't taught to do this at home, school, or work. And, due to our brain's proclivity for distorting reality in our favor, we're actually prone to doing its *opposite*.

Remember, when we're committed to informed choice we work to expand, change, and improve our thinking because we know that, to one degree or another, our mental maps of reality are almost *always* wrong. Except for the simplest of things—like our phone numbers or birthdays—the pictures of reality we carry around in our heads are woefully inadequate, even about the most basic and familiar things. If we hold up the backs of our hands so we can't see them, for example, and then try to describe them perfectly to a person sitting next to us, we can't do it. And if we lack perfect mental maps of the backs of our own hands, how much more imperfect are our views of more complicated, less familiar things?

This begs a question: If we're committed to being well informed, but our perspectives are always riddled with gaps and errors, how do we best detect and correct them? In our quest to make informed and effective choices, how do we check and improve our mental maps of reality?

One thing is clear; given our brains' self-serving biases, it's impossible to effectively test our thinking *with our thinking*—it always looks good. Our minds, after all, want to be right. If testing our thinking with our thinking worked, we could just sit in the lotus position on a yoga mat correcting our thinking before every decision and we'd be in good shape. But given our cognitive limitations, the best way to test our thinking is by bouncing it off other people—especially people with contrasting perspectives.

"The only way that we can be certain that our map of reality is valid is to expose it to the criticism and challenge of other mapmakers," explains M. Scott Peck. "Otherwise we live in a closed system—within a bell jar, to use Sylvia Plath's analogy, rebreathing only our own fetid air, more and more subject to delusion."[5] Without conflicting frames of reference, in other words, we remain trapped in our maps of reality, making biased, less informed choices because we can't correct errors we can't see. So rather than treat our views like truths to be evangelized, we put forward our views— our positions and the thinking behind them—and treat them like *hypotheses* to be tested.

Simple Tests

A good verbal test not only opens the door to contrasting views, it invites them in. When we test our hypotheses, we don't sit back passively and *hope* others will share contrasting perspectives—we actively *encourage* them to disagree, to share how and where they see things differently. After we've put forward our views and explained the thinking behind them, here are a few low-key tests for situations where the barriers to openness are low:

> ➤ Is there a better way to make sense of this?

> ➤ Do you see it differently?

> ➤ How does what I am suggesting feel to you?

> ➤ What's your take on this issue?

> ➤ What does this look like from your angle?

> ➤ What's your reaction to what I've just put forward?

High-Powered Tests

But these casual tests won't serve us well in all circumstances, particularly when the people with whom we're talking face uphill struggles pushing back on our perspectives. If a vice president, for example, is asking a line manager to challenge his point of view, his testing will need to be vigorous enough to encourage the line manager—who is prone to minimize when speaking up the chain of command—to open up and share his real ideas. To that end, let's look at more vigorous tests to employ in situations where it may be more difficult for others to push back, or when we're putting forward a particularly strong perspective:

> ➤ That's how I see the problem. What does the problem look like from your perspective?

> ➤ Right now I feel like my idea makes perfect sense, and that makes me nervous. Are you seeing something I'm missing?

> ➤ I am more interested in making an informed decision than in winning or being right, so I'd like to hear your point of view—especially if it differs from my own.

➤ If I've got a blind spot about this issue, please help me to see it.

➤ I've shared what I think and why I think it. I'm curious to hear how other people are thinking about this problem—especially those who have a different take on it than I do.

➤ To help me improve how I'm looking at this decision, I'd really like to hear from someone who has a perspective that challenges mine.

➤ I'd like someone to expand my view of this situation. Who has a different way of looking at it?

➤ I know I may be wrong about this—what do you think?

➤ If you disagree with me, please let me know. I'd really like to hear your point of view.

➤ Push back on me here—especially if you think I am being unfair.

➤ What would our worst critic say about this decision?

As a conversational manifestation of our commitment to informed choice, testing our view makes a huge difference in how others respond because it signals that we're holding our perspective like a hypothesis, not a truth. Rather than dare people to disagree, we're asking other people for assistance: "Help me improve how I'm looking at this issue."

An executive at a Fortune 500 company provides a superb example of this behavior in action. In a hastily assembled meeting about a major problem facing the project he was leading, he explained to his team his current idea about how to address the problem, and then provided a quick overview of his thinking. He then tested his view; "I'd like to hear from others on this. But if you agree with me right now I don't need to hear from you. I already know what I think. I'd like to spend the limited time we have hearing from those who don't." That's brilliant. Pressed for time, he recognizes he's not going to expand his thinking by listening to people who agree with him, so he leans into difference by encouraging people with different data or interpretations to share how they're looking at the issue. He's not doing this to reach agreement, per se, but to see what their differing views might teach him about the problem so he can make wiser choices about how to address it.

Antitests

This skill is particularly hard to employ when we're being driven by our need to win, but it's exactly what's needed to balance out our fervent candor. As I mentioned earlier, this is not a skill we've grown up using. The sad fact is that after we've put forward a view, we're far more likely to seek self-confirming information by making comments such as these:

> ➤ Who agrees with me?
> ➤ I'm right, yes?
> ➤ Right?
> ➤ You don't see it differently, do you?
> ➤ I know you all agree with me on this.
> ➤ Isn't that so?
> ➤ Don't you agree?
> ➤ It's pretty obvious, isn't it?
> ➤ If anyone disagrees with me, let me know, and I'll explain it again.

By inviting *confirming* views and information, we're giving aid to an already biased brain. The opposite of good tests, these conversational capacity killers push people with differing views out of the conversation. They're antitests that limit our ability to make informed decisions because they protect and reinforce our current thinking rather than subject it to scrutiny.

It's not about being feebleminded. Just because we're testing our views doesn't mean we don't have strong opinions or convictions, it just means we're treating them responsibly—as hypotheses to check and improve rather than truths to protect and sell. "Yes," a workshop participant once said, "this makes sense when I'm concerned my view has problems. But what if I *know* I'm right?"

"Well then," I replied, "if you're that certain your view is correct, you should harbor no reservations about testing it."

Holding our views as hypotheses makes a striking difference in how a team performs. One manager was astonished at how much more information it helped her glean from her team. "At first," she said, "I felt funny testing my views, as if I was insulting my people, like I didn't trust them to speak up." But she was soon shocked to learn how much information had been covered up, watered down, and distorted in her meetings. As she kept up the practice, people increasingly opened up, sharing ideas and concerns to a degree they hadn't previously, bumping her meetings up to a new level of candor and discipline. "I'm very low-key and approachable," she said, "so if they're covering up with me, I can't imagine how closed they're being with the more aggressive managers in this business."

Curiosity Skill 2: Inquiry

There's one more skill that brings full balance to the curiosity side of the conversational scale. Imagine you're in that meeting discussing the important decision with your team. You've put forward a suggestion, explained the thinking behind it, and then tested it: "I'm sure my thinking is off in ways I can't see, so if anyone has a different perspective on this, I'd really like to hear it." No sooner have you asked for pushback than one of your colleague's fires back, "You're kidding, right? That'll never work."

Typically, this is where you lose discipline by arguing or caving in. But if you're on your conversational game, you immediately recognize two things: First, this colleague has earned an A+ for articulating a clear, succinct position (if only a D for tact). Second, you notice what's missing—the underlying thinking that informs *his* position. You know *what* this colleague thinks, but you don't know *why* he thinks it. Because you're aware of what's not being "played," rather than cave in or argue, you seek to understand your colleague's perspective by *inquiring* into the underlying reasons he sees things so differently. You say, "I appreciate your candor, and I want to understand where you're coming from. Can you be specific and provide an example of why you think this won't work?"

When you respond in this way you're demonstrating the fourth skill: genuine *inquiry* into the views of others. When people push back, disagree, put forward a position without explaining it, or simply haven't shared their view at all, we inquire to invite more of their thinking into the conversation. Abraham Lincoln once said, "I don't like that man. I must get to know him better."[6] When someone puts out a view that we don't understand or agree with, rather than get cautious or critical, we adopt Lincoln's attitude and get curious. "I don't like that idea. I should to get to know it better."

It's all about balance. Skilled inquiry is not just asking a single question; it's the *process* of asking as many questions as necessary to get the other person's view into the pool of information being used to make sense of the issue we're addressing. Striking a balance between candor and curiosity, we're working just as hard to get someone else's ideas into the conversation as we are at putting our own views forward—not to win the conversation or minimize conflict, but to improve and expand the available information we're using to make our choices. Our goal isn't agreement, it's understanding.

The hitch, of course, is that it requires tremendous discipline to genuinely inquire into views that conflict with our own. Opposing ideas, particularly about issues we care about, easily trigger our fight-or-flight reactions, leading us to argue our point or withdraw from the conflict. But when our overarching goal is informed choice, we're genuinely curious when others see things differently, recognizing that it's people with different views who are more likely to spark an "aha" moment—the experience of having a blind spot in our mental maps of reality unexpectedly illuminated.

In the hunt for new and conflicting perspectives, we're constantly asking ourselves "aha"-oriented questions: "What do others see that I'm missing? Are they making sense out of things in a way that is more useful than the way I am? How might their perspectives help me detect errors in my own thinking?" Pursuing answers to these questions will often make us uncomfortable and show us we're wrong, but that's the price we must pay if we want to open our eyes to a wider set of realities than those our biased brains naturally filter in.

Responsibility and Discipline

When we put forward our view and *test* it, we're treating it responsibly. When we inquire, we're asking other people to treat *their* views responsibly. When, in a meeting about an important decision, someone blurts out "That's a stupid idea!" we hold that person accountable by asking her to back up her claim. We say, "You might be right; to help us see where you're coming from, would you be willing to describe in more detail why you feel so strongly about it?" We're not shutting people down or giving in, but at the same time, we're not just accepting their claims without some evidence. Are they simply curmudgeons, or do they have perspectives the rest of us haven't considered? There's no way to know unless we ask them to explain their positions.

Higher Expectations

A team that consistently inquires into competing and contrasting views instills more discipline into its work by setting a more rigorous tone. It sets a higher expectation about what it means to participate responsibly in a meeting or discussion. "We're not going to allow flippant comments to derail our meetings," we're saying, in essence. "If you have a view, please share it, but we'll expect you to share your thinking as well. This is a forum for solving problems and making decisions, not for arguing over unsubstantiated opinions. It's a business meeting, not political talk radio."

This brings a refreshing depth and rigor to our interactions with others. We don't mind strong, even antagonistic positions, but we do expect people to explain their reasoning so it can be evaluated. A manager, for instance, responding to a divisive position in a meeting, might react by saying, "That's a contentious viewpoint, Raquel, and I can see the team starting to react. Can you take a few minutes and describe to us what you've seen or heard that leads you to think that?" Inquiring in this way holds Raquel accountable for her view, allows the rest of the team access to her thinking, and helps the team remain sharply focused on making the most informed choice possible.

Inquiry Pulls a Team Back to the Sweet Spot

A great example of how inquiry can simultaneously pull a team back to the sweet spot, facilitate deeper learning, and hold people accountable for their views—even when they're being hostile—comes from my brother Randy, a sixth-grade teacher in Southern California. A few years back he had a girl with special needs, Julia, mainstreamed into his class. Julia's mother was infamous for her relentless complaining about the caliber of the education her child was receiving in regular elementary school classrooms. Since Julia had started kindergarten, parent-teacher conferences had been stressful and combative, and the tensions between the mother and the school were high.

When the parents requested a meeting with the teacher and administration to discuss Julia's progress, my brother was well aware that this mother was difficult, but he had no idea that the parent-teacher conference was such a concern for the principal. On the day of the conference, the principal, wanting to protect Randy from the wrath of Julia's mother, unilaterally decided to present a "show of force." Attending the conference to support my brother was the principal, the district psychologist, a member of the district administration, and my brother's teaching assistant.

When the mother arrived, she brought with her the girl's father, and it was he who opened the session with a verbal salvo: "I'm sick and tired of you giving my daughter bad grades because you don't like the relationship my wife has with this school," he barked at my brother, directly accusing him of grade retribution.

The district psychologist, knowing nothing of the skills we've been exploring, attempted to defend Randy by contesting the accusation: "I don't think that is what's happening here, I think . . ."

"I'm not talking to you," the father snapped, cutting her off midsentence.

Randy, who is very familiar with these skills, waited until he had a chance to speak and then *leaned into* the accusation with an inquiry: "You've said that I'm giving Julia grades as retribution for your wife's relationship with the school. I'm curious, what signals are you seeing from me that lead you to think that's what's happening here?"

The husband, caught off guard by being asked to explain his point, looked over at his wife and said, "Honey, what *are* we seeing from the teacher?"

"Well, what else could it be?" said the mother, "He gave her a C." As Randy inquired further, neither parent could provide any data to back up their claims. They'd jumped to negative conclusions about their daughter's grades based on the *absence* of data. When it became clear that they could provide no evidence of grade retribution, my brother simply said, "If you don't mind, let me explain, from my vantage point as her teacher, why your daughter's getting these grades. Once I lay it all out, I'd like to hear your thoughts and reactions." My brother shared samples of Julia's work, talked about her progress, and described how Julia's emotional problems affected her learning. He also explained his philosophy of teaching special-needs children. "I will not grade-inflate," he said. "I know many teachers do, believing that it helps the child's self-esteem. But I think it's a poor educational strategy, and I won't do it. Julia will always get the grades she earns in my class, and I believe that's the best long-term approach. So we may just have a difference of opinion here; you see her current grades as a problem, but I see them as kind of heroic. She's put a lot of work into those grades. I think you should be proud of her," he said. "That is my take on what's happening with your daughter's grades. What's your reaction to what I've just put on the table?"

"I like everything you've just told me," replied the father. "I've just never heard any of this before."

"That's because we've never talked," said my brother. "In the future, please call or drop by whenever you have a question or concern," as he slid his contact information across the table. "Is there anything I can do differently so we don't let future misunderstandings get this far again?"

Randy's handling of this conversation is impressive. Neither accepting the accusation at face value nor dismissing it, he defused the explosive situation by getting curious. By *inquiring* into the underlying reasoning behind the assertion, he brought the conversation back to a more balanced, data-based dialogue, pulling a tense and divisive parent-teacher conference right back to the sweet spot.

Sample Inquiries

Here is a list of sample inquiries—a starter kit, if you will. I encourage you to find ways of putting these in your own words so they sound natural coming from you. When someone states a position but fails to back it up with his or her thinking, we might respond in one of the following ways:

> ➤ What are you seeing that leads you to that view?

> ➤ I have to admit that I see the issue very differently, but before I jump to conclusions, please tell me what you have seen or heard that leads you to see it the way you do.

> ➤ Tell me more about how you're looking at this issue.

> ➤ Obviously, you're looking at this differently. Help me see this through your lens. How are you making sense of X?

> ➤ What does this look like from your (marketing/finance/engineering) perspective?

> ➤ Help me expand my thinking on this. Tell me how you see X.

> ➤ What have you seen or heard that leads you to think X?

> ➤ Can you provide a couple of examples that illustrate your position?

> ➤ Clearly, we don't agree. Let's see what our different perspectives can teach us about this issue. Explain in more detail how you're seeing the situation.

> I'm intrigued by the way you're framing this issue. Can you give an additional example or two so I can better understand your thinking?

> Can you give me an example of X?

> Can you illustrate why you see this so differently than I do?

When team members haven't even shared their positions, much less their thinking, and we want to invite their perspectives into the conversation, we might say:

> We've been bouncing this idea around for quite some time, and we haven't heard from you yet. As you've been listening to the pros and cons of this decision, what's your take on the best choice?

> Are you seeing anything that the rest of us may have missed?

> I'd be interested in hearing your views on this problem. Do you have a different perspective than those that have already been shared?

Don't Ask Why

Asking "Why?" is a poor way to inquire into someone's thinking because it invites a response that provides little additional data or clarification. For example, suppose someone comments, "Bob should not be given this project, he can't handle it." If you simply ask "Why?" the response could be, "I just don't think he's up to it."

Merely asking "why" produced no additional insight, just a rehashed version of the same vague position. A more effective inquiry encourages people to share the underlying reasoning they hold their positions: "What have you seen or heard that leads you to feel that way about Bob and this project?"

To this the person might respond, "Bob's daughter has some serious health issues right now, and a lot of his time and energy is being spent with her." This more effective inquiry generates a far clearer and more accurate understanding of the colleague's reservations about Bob.

A Few Poor Inquiries

It's important to note that inquiry is more than just asking a question. A genuine inquiry comes from a place of curiosity, while a disingenuous question can stem from anything from contempt to disbelief. Consider these examples of poor inquiries and just plain nasty ones:

> ➤ You don't really think that do you?
> ➤ Is that the best you can do?
> ➤ Why the hell do you think that?
> ➤ Do you have a learning impediment?

Testing and Inquiry: What's the Difference?

Like the previous skills, mastering inquiry is more difficult than it may appear, for it requires that we maintain an inquisitive mind in circumstances where our minds usually slam shut—in the face of strong conflict, disagreement, tension, and discord. There's another reason this skill is a challenge. When people first begin using these skills, they're often confused over the distinction between a *test* and an *inquiry*. They ask, "What's the difference? They're both just asking questions, right?" While both skills are a form of asking questions, we separate them out as distinct skills because they serve unique functions: We test our own hypotheses. We *inquire* into the hypotheses of others.

One last note about the curiosity skills. When we first start testing and inquiring in a more consistent way, especially if this new behavior runs counter to our traditional ways of talking with others, it helps to explain *why* we're inquiring and testing so our colleagues are less likely to misunderstand our intentions by saying something like, "I am not asking you for input because I want to argue or shut you down. I really want to see how you're looking at this issue because it might improve how I'm looking at it."

Before We Move On

In the last chapter we explored a mindset that provides a more enlightened way of *thinking* in a conversation. In this chapter we've explored a set of skills that provide a more disciplined way of participating in a conversation under pressure—balancing candor and curiosity in the genuine pursuit of informed and effective choice.

The Sweet Spot

"Minimizing" (Low Candor) ←——— ● ———→ *(Low Curiosity) "Winning"*

or

Position and Thinking (Candor) ——→ ● ←—— *(Curiosity) Testing and Inquiry*

I'm sure you have many questions. In the chapters that follow we'll explore these skills in more detail, including when to use them, when not to, and how they support decision making, problem solving, and other important activities. We'll also explore strategies for using our daily work as a dojo for building our facility with these skills, as well as unique ideas about the connection between conversational capacity and team leadership.

Deceptively simple in theory, these skills are challenging in practice—our minimize and win tendencies guarantee it. But the practice is worth it. As we acquire the discipline to balance candor and curiosity under pressure, we dramatically improve our conversations and meetings because we avoid the dysfunctional ends of the behavioral spectrum. With our internal compass pointed toward informed choice, we respond to conflict, dissent, or disagreement in an open, balanced, learning-focused way.

Imagine a team full of such people.

Now imagine an organization full of such teams.

Cultivating Our Better Angels

....

Human nature is the problem,
but human nature is also the solution.

STEVEN PINKER

"**L**et your principles be few and simple," advised the Greek philosopher Epictetus, "so that you may refer to them at a moment's notice." The mindset and skills we explored in the last two chapters provide just that—a user-friendly set of principles for working in the sweet spot under pressure. The skills are simple:

1. Candor skills

   ➤ Advocate your *position* clearly and succinctly.

   ➤ Illustrate your position by sharing the *thinking* behind it (both your data and your interpretation).

2. Curiosity skills

   ➤ *Test* your views. Seek out what you might be missing. Encourage others to share views that contrast with yours. Hunt for disconfirming information.

➤ *Inquire* into the views of others and actively explore their thinking, especially when their perspectives differ from your own.

The balanced use of these four skills keeps us grounded in the sweet spot. When we fail to employ the two candor skills, we begin to minimize. When we fail to test and inquire, we start to "win."

"All Push, No Pull"

To see this framework in action, let's go back to the human Flamethrower. In the workshop he attended, he pointed at these four skills on the flip chart and declared, "That's my problem right there. I'm all push, no pull." He explained that while he was very good at "pushing" his views on others, "I don't lift a finger to get anyone else's way of looking at things into a meeting. It's no wonder I'm considered difficult." This was a revelation. He'd never seen the problem so clearly.

Armed with his newfound insight, the Flamethrower worked hard to participate in meetings in a more disciplined, balanced way. He did this by testing his own views and by inquiring into the views of his colleagues to counterbalance his natural "push" style. But, despite his efforts, his teammates were reluctant to share their own views or to push back on those of the Flamethrower. Why? They simply didn't trust him. His new approach ran counter to his historical behavior, and, compounding the problem, his use of the new skills came across as mechanical and inauthentic. Rather than flow from him naturally (as did his position and his thinking), his testing and inquiry seemed scripted and contrived. "When he asks for our input," one of his colleagues told me, "he sounds like he's reading from a cue card."

A couple of months later I was back on site, working with another team, and I ran into one of the Flamethrower's teammates.

"How's the team doing?" I inquired.

"Much better," he said.

"What changed? You guys were really stuck at first. How did you break through it?"

"It was the Flamethrower," he replied, "It was actually quite remarkable. At first, he was testing and inquiring in meetings, trying to pull us into the discussion, but no one really believed him, so no one would take him up on it. Then he'd start getting frustrated, which made us even more reluctant to jump in. So you're right, we were kind of stuck. But then we started to see something that surprised us," he added. "He started showing up at our offices after meetings, bringing us a cup of coffee, saying, 'Can we talk? It might have been hard to say something in the meeting, but I'd really like to hear what you think about this.'"

These four skills were not a magic pill. The Flamethrower had to demonstrate that he meant it. When his teammates saw that he was so genuinely interested in hearing their ideas that he was memorizing their coffee preferences and seeking them out on their own turf, it signaled that his *mindset*, not just his behavior, was truly changing.

But Won't I Look Weak?

Achieving balance is the objective. To become more effective, we don't water down an existing strength; we build new skills to balance it out. The Flamethrower didn't stop being candid, he just learned to balance his natural candor by testing and inquiring.

"But if I test my view, won't I look weak?" I'm often asked. The answer to that question depends, of course, on our definition of strength. If we think being strong means sticking to our own narrow view, no matter how flawed it may be, and closing ourselves off to improving it, then yes, this approach will make us look very weak indeed. But this puerile notion of strength reminds me of Stephen Colbert's humorous observation at the White House Correspondents' Dinner in 2006: "When the president decides something on Monday, he still believes it on Wednesday, no matter what happened Tuesday."[1] But pigheadedly sticking to a point of view is not a sign of strength; it's a symptom of weakness. Any dolt can shut down or argue when he or she is being challenged, but it requires real strength to remain open to learning, squarely focused on informed choice, even when we're feeling stressed and vulnerable. Our capacity to rein in our derailing tendencies in circumstances where other people cannot is a sign that we're in disciplined control of our behavior and not a piteous slave to our emotional reactions.

When Should These Skills Be Used?

Do our conversations *always* need to be so rigorous? The answer, of course, is no. In situations where it's easy to align our behavior and our intentions, there's no need for such deliberate structure. It would be absurd, for instance, if we said to a friend, "I think it's a beautiful day outside. Let me share my thinking with you, and then I'd like to get your reaction." It's a *casual* conversation. Too much rigor defeats the purpose. By the same token, in a crisis, as when there's a fire in the building, balanced dialogue isn't appropriate either; we simply need to direct people to safety.

But a more mindful and deliberate approach is important when we're facing difficult topics, tough decisions, intense conflicts, or other challenges where our minimize and win (min–win) tendencies are likely to work against our intentions. So, when we're deciding whether to address an issue, we should ask ourselves a couple of basic questions and plan accordingly:

1. How *difficult* is the issue?

2. How *important* is it?

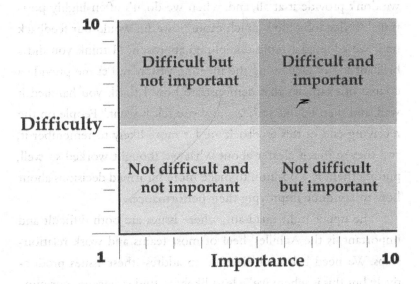

These two questions create a simple way to assess where we should use the skills, and, just as important, where we shouldn't. We should avoid conversations, for example, in the upper left quadrant. Frustrating and futile, this is high pain–low gain territory that includes such things as arguing about politics or religion. In the lower left quadrant, where the conversations are neither difficult nor important, there's no need for lots of structure. We do just fine chatting about things like how we spent our weekend, the latest book we've read, or a brilliant play in last night's ball game.

As we move to the right, we enter the "high importance" side of the grid. In the lower right quadrant, we have discussions that are not too difficult, but they're worth having. These conversations are perfect for practicing the cadence and rhythm of this balanced approach to dialogue because, with something worthwhile at stake, the issue is worth the extra discipline, but it's not so difficult that our min-win tendencies pose a big threat.

Providing positive feedback is a great example. All too often, we don't provide it at all, and, when we do, it's often highly positional: "Nice job." How much more powerful would our feedback be if we adopted a more disciplined approach? "I think you did a brilliant job of facilitating the meeting yesterday. Let me provide a couple of examples that demonstrate how I think you handled it well, and then I'd like to hear how you felt it went." People on the receiving end of this feedback are far more likely to remember it, and they're much clearer about what we thought worked so well, putting them in a position to make more informed decisions about how to continue improving their performance.

The upper right quadrant, where issues are both difficult and important, is the Achilles' heel of most teams and work relationships. We need balanced dialogue to address these issues productively, but this is where we're least likely to find it, because our min-win tendencies are vibrating at high frequency. Practice is essential in this quadrant, too, but in a different way. Even a highly skilled practitioner may need to prepare for these challenging conversations ahead of time. As we prepare, essential questions to explore include: What is my position on this issue? What examples can I find to clearly illustrate it? What would be a good way to test it? How might the other person react, and how can I use inquiry to manage those reactions productively?

For a really challenging conversation—a 10/10 (rated 10 on the difficulty scale and 10 on importance)—there is no substitute for practicing with a partner. By having a colleague play the person with whom we need to have the conversation, we can more realistically assess and improve our ability to maintain conversational discipline. When it comes to practicing these skills, role playing makes the same difference as between talking about playing tennis and actually picking up a racket and hitting the ball. A partner will see things we're missing and can help us fine-tune our approach *before* we have the real conversation, significantly increasing our ability to remain balanced when it counts. Is our position clear? Are we providing enough of our thinking to explain our position? Is our test strong enough? Are we using inquiry to manage a variety of possible responses, or are we sliding right back to our old habits? The best way to find answers to these questions is to ask someone to help us prepare.

The basic rule is this: The more important and challenging the conversation we're facing, the higher the conversational capacity we need to engage it. If there's a gap between our current skill level and the difficulty of the conversation we're facing, we use practice to help bridge the gap.

What If I'm Cut Off?

If we're afraid team members might cut us off before we get a chance to share our thinking and test it, we can alert them ahead of time that they'll have an opportunity to respond and that we're curious to hear their perspectives: "Let me tell you what I think and explain why I think it, and then I'd like to hear what *you* think, especially if you see things differently."

By letting them know we're going to put forward our own view and then ask for their reactions to it, we decrease the likelihood that they'll cut us off because they know they'll be invited to respond. And if they cut us off anyway, we can remind them of the protocol we're trying to follow: "I do want to hear your thoughts and reactions, but give me a minute or two to share my thinking with you so you can respond more effectively to how I'm looking at the issue."

It Takes Time

As we build our discipline for working in the sweet spot, we're seeking the yin and yang of dialogue by being bold, authentic, and direct and, simultaneously, open-minded, unpretentious, and inquisitive. Our balanced demeanor signals that we're not going to let our ego get in the way of the best choice. Because it forces us to consciously sacrifice our base tendencies to something less egocentric, this discipline, as a colleague of mine put it, is "a direct assault on narcissism."[2]

Adopting this more balanced approach is not something that happens overnight. It's a gradual process that requires ongoing practice; our mindset shifts as we use the skills, and our skill level grows as our mindset shifts. An HR executive I've known for years provides a great description of his experience with this learning process. As a strong minimizer in a team of executives sporting strong win tendencies, he had a hard time holding his own in meetings and conversations. But, by using the four skills, he was able to dramatically change how he participated in meetings.

"At first," he explained, "I progressed from rarely putting forward my views at all to actually stating my view and then testing it. But when I first started, I noticed that after testing my perspective, I'd wince and hold my breath for fear that someone might actually disagree. So I was testing, but not really in the true spirit of it. I was doing it because I knew I should—not because I really *meant* it." But he stuck with the practice. "After a few weeks I suddenly noticed my emotional reaction had changed. After testing an idea, I'd be really *curious* to see if anyone had a different thought. That was a big shift for me, but it didn't stop there," he said. "I now find that I'm actually *disappointed* when no one challenges how I'm looking at things. It's a letdown. Agreement isn't very interesting."

With practice, he evolved from seeing disagreement as a threat to seeing it as a source of learning, of fun, the source of the "aha" in a conversation. "It's funny," he added. "I used to be concerned that people *would* disagree with me. Now I'm more concerned when they *don't*."

Consensus?

In my workshops, another question frequently asked is this: "Do we just talk until we agree? Is this a tool for consensus decision making? At what point do we break off the conversation and actually *do* something?"

"Good question," I say. "Tell me what your decision-making protocol is, and I'll tell you how this discipline can enhance it." By bringing more balance and rigor to conversations and getting our ego out of the mix, this discipline enhances all manner of decision making. If our manager is going to make the decision, for instance, we can use these skills to help her improve her thinking. This is how Lincoln operated. He didn't run his team of rivals by consensus. He made the tough calls, but he used his team to help expand, improve, and adjust his thinking before he made an important decision.

When a consensus decision is the best option, a more balanced approach helps to level the playing field. It's far harder for the team member with the strong win tendency to run away with the decision if the team has the capacity to work in the sweet spot. And when a manager must make a quick decision without input—as in a crisis—he can use this more structured approach to explain *why* he's made the decision (so team members don't misunderstand the logic behind his decision) and to *engage* the team in finding the most efficient and effective way to implement the decision.

In short, these skills are a way of orchestrating balanced dialogue; they're not a decision-making process. But by bolstering a team's conversational capacity, they help whoever is making the decision make it with a far more informed perspective. When we're focused on informed choice, the question we should always have in our head is, "Who are we helping to make the decision?" If we don't know the answer to that question, it should spark our first inquiry: "Before we begin exploring this issue, I'd like to make sure I understand the objective; what is the decision we're going to make, and who are we helping to make it?"

Isn't It Just a Matter of Trust?

I've been told many times, "This is all about trust. If we just had more trust in our team, we could talk about our bigger issues." But high conversational capacity is not the product of high trust. Remember the executive team in Silicon Valley. The team members liked, trusted, and respected one another, yet they regularly sacrificed candor to avoid spoiling the team's collegial atmosphere. Trust isn't like pizza, something we can just order in when we feel like it. So if it's the key to high conversational capacity, and our capacity is low, we face a conundrum: we need high trust to build our conversational capacity, but we can't build our conversational capacity with low trust. We're stuck.

But that's the wrong way to think about it. Trust isn't a *prerequisite* for effective conversations; it's the *product* of effective conversations. "If you could learn to work together in more effective and trustworthy ways, you could simultaneously solve some of your problems and start building back the trust," I tell teams. If trust is the product of how team members interact with each other, then *it's by building more trustworthy relationships that we generate higher trust*. The key to building high levels of trust in a team, in other words, is to have increasingly trustworthy conversations. So how do we do this?

Cultivating Our "Better Angels"

Our troublesome fight-flight tendencies are primal, base aspects of our being. But they're an innate part of our behavioral repertoire, and they serve us well in limited circumstances, so we can't just get rid of them. We can, however, learn to put them in their place. As we build our discipline for working in the sweet spot, we can reduce their impact on our behavior by intentionally cultivating higher aspects of our humanity—what Abraham Lincoln referred to as the "better angels of our nature."[3] When we set aside our urges to minimize and put forward our positions and thinking, we exercise both *candor* and *courage*. Turning our backs on our need to win by testing and inquiring, on the other hand, is an exercise in *curiosity* and *humility*.

It takes guts to candidly express our thoughts when every fiber of our being is telling us to be cautious. If we have a strong minimize tendency, for instance, clearly advocating our view when we're worried about the reaction it may incite can provoke a fear response akin to a fear of public speaking or bungee jumping. Speaking up anyway, even as every fiber of our being is telling us not to, is an act of courage.

On the other side of the scale, testing a perspective we hold dear is a humble act. It takes modesty to admit our view may be missing something, that it may be *wrong*. But humility is exactly what's needed to counter our vain need to be right. In a similar way, genuinely inquiring into a contrary view demonstrates a high degree of curiosity, indicating we're more interested in exploring divergent ideas than in being comfortable or right.

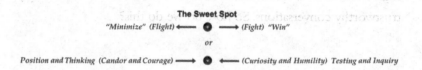

The Sweet Spot

"Minimize" (Flight) ←——— ● ———→ *(Fight) "Win"*

or

Position and Thinking (Candor and Courage) ———→ ● ←——— *(Curiosity and Humility) Testing and Inquiry*

Again, we can never fully escape our compulsion to minimize and win, but we can reduce the power these predilections have on our behavior with a two-pronged strategy. First, by ignoring the siren song of these primal tendencies and resisting the urge to indulge in the habitual behaviors they trigger, we can let them atrophy from lack of use. Second, by learning to balance candor and courage with curiosity and humility, we can cultivate the better angels of our nature, making them increasingly ascendant. With regular practice, in other words, we essentially starve our old habits and feed our new ones.

How We're "Being" in a Conversation

If the mindset refocuses how we're *thinking* in a conversation, and the skillset shifts what we're *doing*, these higher aspects of our nature transform how we're *being* in the conversation. And while we don't need to structure every conversation so rigorously, it makes sense to generally adopt this way of "being." Balancing candor and courage with curiosity and humility is a good way to walk down the path of life. I can't think of a situation where it wouldn't be a useful way to *be* in the moment. Can you?

This is the real secret to building more effective teams and work relationships: it's not in what we're thinking or doing but in how we're *being*, standing firm in the sweet spot, tempering our base tendencies with our better angels. We're less defensive and more open because any challenge to our thinking provokes a candid and curious response, not a defensive one. We're more genuinely interested in making informed choices than in mollycoddling our egos, and our attitudes and behavior reflect it. By bringing our higher selves to important conversations and decisions, we provoke less defensiveness in others, thereby encouraging them to bring forward their best efforts and thinking. The key to building trustworthy work relationships, in other words, is increasing our conversational capacity.

The Humble CEO

It's not about being perfect. The path to mastery is a strenuous, slippery, high-altitude climb. We'll often slip, let go of candor, and become overly guarded and cautious. Other times we'll lose our footing, drop curiosity, and grow more arrogant and argumentative. This is okay. It's a natural part of the learning process, not a sign we're failing, or uncommitted to lasting change. Having stumbled, we merely stand back up, dust ourselves off, and try again, seeing the mishap as another opportunity to learn about our tendencies and how to better manage them. We're motivated to invest in this ongoing effort because we're aware of the fundamental choice before us. In our daily interactions with other people we're constantly strengthening certain aspects of our character. We know our only choice is which aspects we choose to cultivate: conformity and timidity, or candor and courage? Arrogance and ignorance, or curiosity and humility?

The experience of a feisty CEO of a healthcare organization demonstrates that the choice to exercise our better angels and rein in a long-established habit is no trivial undertaking. At a break during one of my workshops he came up to me and said,

"My need to win is out of control. I've beaten the will to disagree completely out of my executive team," he confessed. "I've turned them into a bunch of butt-kissing sycophants who won't confront me to save a patient's life." In the conversation that followed, he went on to say, "My need to get my way isn't just a problem at work. I have two children who live with an ex-wife, and I am in the middle of my third ugly divorce." Frustration radiated off him like heat waves off a desert highway on a summer day. "I'm so sick of the relationship thing," he said, "that the next time around I've decided to shortcut the process by finding a woman I hate and buying her a house."

As the workshop progressed and we explored the four skills, he latched onto the "all push, no pull" idea. "That's exactly my problem," he said. Armed with this new insight, he shared the framework with his team, and then, like the Flamethrower, began testing and inquiring to balance out his traditional "push" style.

A couple of weeks later I received a phone call. "It's not working," boomed the CEO.

"Tell me more," I said, "What leads you to think it's not working?"

It became clear that he was running up against the same two barriers that had frustrated the Flamethrower, namely, trust and skill. His new behaviors contradicted his past behavior, and because he was still learning the new skills, when he tested and inquired it wasn't as natural or authentic as the team would have preferred. So his team members responded with deep suspicion, neither sharing their views nor pushing back on those of their CEO. Working hard to change his behavior, and unaccustomed to failure, he grew frustrated that his efforts weren't paying off and quickly snapped back to his old, familiar habits. That's when he called me.

"You've explained to the team what you're trying to do, and you're actively following through in meetings with more testing and inquiry," I said. "Yet the team still isn't responding. What, in your mind, is getting in the way?" The tone of his response suggested he thought I was a moron for asking the question: "Are you kidding? It's seems obvious to me. They think I'm trying to pull them into the open for a cleaner shot."

In the conversation that followed, I discovered the CEO was using "blanket" tests. After putting forward a position and explaining it, he'd ask, "Does anyone have a different view?" Because he called on no one in particular, the blanket test made it easy for each of his executives to dodge the question. To remedy this, I suggested he do more focused testing, calling on specific people to push back on his views: "Jim, you tend to see things differently than I do. What is your reaction to what I just put on the table?" or "Kiyoko, what does your finance background tell you about this decision?"

The CEO decided to take it even further. In their next team meeting, he showed just how serious he was about changing the dynamic in the group. "I have been trying to change the way I work with you by doing more testing and inquiring, but you don't trust me. To be honest, I don't blame you. I don't even trust myself yet. I'm not good at this," he said. "But we can't just wait for the trust to arrive," he continued, "So I'm making a new rule. I'll continue to put my thoughts on the table and explain them. Once I've done that, I want to go around the room and hear from everyone at the table. No one gets a pass, and I don't want to hear anything positive. You've all got to take a shot at my thinking. That is going to be hard for me to take, and I know it'll be even harder for you to do. I just don't know how else to undo what I've done to this team."

There's the humility.

As with the Flamethrower, the team members began to realize that their CEO's mindset, not just his behavior, was undergoing a transformative shift. It wasn't an easy path for the team to take, and there were more than a few setbacks along the way, but over the next few months the CEO put tremendous effort into managing his behavior more effectively, and in the process, he cultivated a healthier and more disciplined team.

It's a Conversational Martial Art

Our ability to mindfully resist the pull of our minimize and win tendencies and maintain intentional balance is the measure of our conversational capacity. Developing the discipline to pull this off is no simple matter. It's not a gimmick we can master overnight, it's a conversational martial art, and if we want to earn a black belt—able to stay open, balanced, and learning focused under the toughest of circumstances—it takes lots of practice.

The danger in framing it as a martial art is that it may tempt some people to think, "Great. I can use it against my colleagues." But in this martial art, the person with whom we're talking isn't our opponent. The conversation, and the person with whom we're having it, merely provides the mat on which the contest takes place. In this martial art our opponent is our own ego and the fierce emotional reactions that protect it. When it comes to conversational capacity, ego is the enemy of effectiveness.

Seen in this light, improving how we converse with others offers a path to personal transformation, a way to become less ego driven and more purpose driven. It offers us a new way to think about teams and teamwork—as an opportunity to become more balanced human beings—simultaneously forthright and authentic, yet unpretentious and open-minded. And here's the good news: we get paid to practice. When it comes to building our competence, *the workplace is our dojo*—an ideal practice space for building and refining our skills.

The Work Is Worth It

It's not just about personal development. As we kick our egos to the curb and focus on informed choice, our definition of effectiveness expands beyond the borders of our own narrow thoughts and needs. As we focus our energies on growing our teams' capacities for working in the sweet spot, our goal is to foster a culture of growth, learning, and competence—a workplace that is open and fair, where informed decision making is the superordinate goal and useful information and ideas are quickly utilized, no matter their source. Handling our disagreements, conflicts, and differences in a disciplined, balanced way, we create an upsurge of trust and respect, even between people who may never be best of friends outside the office.

In such a workplace, our interactions are governed by a refreshing set of values. Rather than let whoever has the most authority or the biggest mouth "win," we operate as a meritocracy governed by a more principled credo: "Everyone who helps orchestrate a conversation that leads to the best idea, wins." And as our conversational capacity goes up, our team becomes more agile and innovative, for as John Kao, the author of *Jamming* and an expert on innovation and creativity, points out, it's "new stimuli, challenging input, and dissonant opinions that form the raw materials of the creative process."[4]

We become the active architects of our work environment rather than its passive victims, creating "a culture that brings every mind into the game,"[5] where the experience and thinking of all people is valued, pulled into the process, and utilized. We foster an environment that encourages people to bring their best selves to work, a workplace that is as good for people as it is for the business, that rewards people who put forward their best efforts and discourages those who put their egos ahead of learning and effectiveness.

The result is a team and organization that attracts smart, motivated, experienced people and encourages them to bring their best efforts to the tasks at hand, to the benefit of all stakeholders: employees, shareholders, customers, and communities. It creates a culture that is increasingly good for people and for business—no matter what business we're in.

Conversational Capacity and the Value of Conflict

....

Five senses; an incurably abstract intellect;
a haphazardly selective memory;
a set of preconceptions and assumptions
so numerous that I can never examine more
than a minority of them—never become
even conscious of them all. How much of total
reality can such an apparatus let through?

C. S. LEWIS

Now that we're five chapters into the book, let's pause and consider a couple of questions: Is conversational capacity really such a big game changer in building high-performance teams? Is it really the decisive variable when it comes to working together in tough, adaptive circumstances? These are fair questions, and in this chapter I'll explain why the answer to both questions is an unassailable yes, for teams with high conversational capacity enjoy a profound competence unavailable to less disciplined teams: the ability to transform base conflict into learning gold—a game-changing ability that converts a traditional source of team weakness into a pivotal source of team strength.

What Is Your Mind Doing?

To explore this in more detail, let's start with a story. A few years ago, I asked a group of high school students to read these four simple sentences:

> *A businessman had just turned off the lights in the store when a man appeared and demanded money. The owner opened a cash register. The contents of the cash register were scooped up, and the man sped away. A member of the police force was notified promptly.*[1]

I then asked them to rate a series of statements about the story as true, false, or unknowable. The statements included:

➤ A man appeared after the owner had turned off his store lights.

➤ The robber was a man.

➤ The man who opened the cash register was the owner.

Because the story is deliberately ambiguous, the students had varying interpretations of the events, and they quickly began to argue with each other over their conflicting answers. It was fantastic.

After the class calmed down and we reviewed the answers, I asked the students a few questions about the exercise: "So what does this tell you about how your mind works?"

"We jump to conclusions," several students blurted out.

"That's exactly right," I responded. "So let me ask you this: Did your mind *tell you* it was going to jump to those conclusions?"

"No," the students responded.

"Did a little red warning light go off in your head letting you know when your mind was jumping to a conclusion?"

"No," they again answered, their reflective tone suggesting they were pondering the question's implications.

"Well then, at the very least, when you got up this morning and looked in the mirror, did you give your mind *permission* to jump to conclusions?"

"No," they again replied.

I then asked, "So, what else is your mind doing without your permission?"

"*I don't know,*" was the alarmed reply.

It's a good question. What is our mind doing without our permission? The answer, when you look into it, is that it's doing a lot.

The City Street

Consider the experience of two men visiting Chicago for the first time. Traveling together to attend a meeting, they land at O'Hare airport and share a taxi into town. Arriving early, they decide to wander the streets together and explore the downtown area. An hour later, as they walk into their meeting, the woman who summoned them to Chicago, knowing it's their first visit, asks them a question, "What do you think of the city?"

"It's a dump," exclaims one.

"It's beautiful," raves the other.

One question we might ask is, "Who is *right?*" But that's not the most interesting line of inquiry. (I'm not even sure what "right" has to do with it. It's like going to an art gallery and asking the curator, "Which painting is right?") A more compelling question to consider is this: "Why did they each *see* the city so differently?"

The Ladder of Inference

Their conflicting views of Chicago can be explained by exploring the "ladder of inference,"[2] a popular concept developed by Chris Argyris that illustrates how the mind makes sense of its experience. At the bottom rung of the ladder is the directly observable data, all the sensory inputs available to these men as they stroll up a city street—the vast array of things they can see, smell, taste, hear, or feel, all the directly observable data.

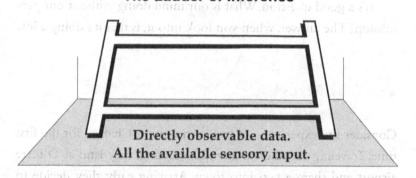

The Ladder of Inference

**Directly observable data.
All the available sensory input.**

Because of their cognitive limitations—the human mind can't focus on everything going on around it at once—they're forced to move up to the next rung on the ladder by paying attention to some aspects of the city and ignoring others. So, while there are an unfathomable number of things they can observe as they walk up a city street, they're only able to focus on a small sliver of them. If one man zeros in on the fancy Thai restaurant across the street, for instance, he may not notice the man by the subway playing Bach on the banjo.

The Ladder of Inference

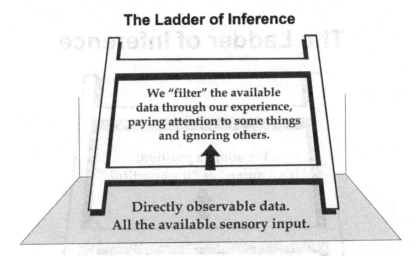

We "filter" the available data through our experience, paying attention to some things and ignoring others.

Directly observable data.
All the available sensory input.

Continuing up the ladder, the narrow sliver of things on which they each focus leads them to make very different *inferences*, or assumptions, about the city. It is each man's unique combination of data and inferences that lead them to adopt such contradictory *positions* about the city: One thinks it's a dump. The other thinks it's beautiful.

The net effect of their ascent up differing ladders is profound. If we put a GPS unit on these two men, we could definitively declare, "They're in *exactly* the same place." But if we could look inside their heads and see what they're each experiencing, we'd be forced to admit, "They're nowhere near each other."

Our Brain Is a Filter

The reason they're "nowhere near each other" is simple. As these men explore the city, their unique cultural, educational, experiential backgrounds lead them to *filter* the available sensory input in very different ways. "No man ever looks at the world with pristine

The Ladder of Inference

We adopt a position:
"It's a dump" or "It's beautiful."

We make inferences,
assumptions, and interpretations
to make sense of the
sliver of data we've selected.

We "filter" the available
data through our experience,
paying attention to some things
and ignoring others.

Directly observable data.
All the available sensory input.

eyes," said anthropologist Ruth Benedict. "He sees it edited by a definite set of customs and institutions and ways of thinking."[3] If one of these men grew up on a farm in rural Iowa, for example, he'd experience the city differently from someone who grew up on the Upper East Side of Manhattan. So even though they're walking up the same city street, much of what they could pay attention to is, as Robert Pirsig put it, "cut off by cultural filtering."[4]

Our emotional state is another factor that determines how we go up the ladder. We all know how vastly different the world appears when we're in a foul mood or a great one. And as anyone who's learned a second language knows, the language we speak is yet another powerful filter of our experience. Anthropologist Clyde Kluckhohn explains it thusly:

> Any language is more than an instrument of conveying ideas, more even than an instrument for working upon the feelings of others and for self-expression. Every language is also a means of categorizing experience. The events of the "real" world are never felt or reported as a machine would do it. There is a selection process and an interpretation in the very act of response. Some features of the external situation are highlighted, others are ignored or not fully discriminated. . . . The language says, as it were, "Notice this," "Always consider this separate from that," or "Such and such things always belong together." Since persons are trained from infancy to respond in these ways they take such discriminations for granted as part of the inescapable stuff of life.[5]

Our vocational training is still another potent filter. It's easier to understand how these two men climbed such different ladders of inference, for example, when I reveal that one of them is a cop, the other, an architect. As a result of their vocational differences (not to mention any differences in personality, cultural background, or life experience), they each filter the city very differently. Walking up the city street, the cop's attention naturally gravitates to people, graffiti, gang attire, prison tattoos, and suspicious behavior. If he's had traffic duty, he notices double-parked cars, expired parking meters, expired registration tags, jaywalkers, rolling stops, and the running of red lights. He doesn't have to work hard to focus on all this—he can't even help it. His ascent up the ladder is so skilled and automatic that he's largely unaware of the degree to which his mind is filtering his experience of the city.

Strolling down the same street right next to the cop, the architect's attention goes in a markedly different direction. His narrow band of focus centers on buildings, materials, historical landmarks, and design. As he saunters, wide-eyed, around the most architecturally significant city in the United States, he's like a kid in a toy store.

So when they declare their positions on the city—"It's a dump," and "It's beautiful"—each is doing so perched on top of his unique ladder of inference, largely unaware that there are more expansive ways of experiencing the city. As Robert Pirsig so eloquently put it, "We take a handful of sand from the endless landscape of awareness around us and call that handful of sand the world."[6] The positions adopted by the cop and the architect aren't wrong, they're just incomplete, because they each grabbed a different handful of awareness from the streets of Chicago around them and called *their* handful of awareness "the city."

Cognitive Cartography

The "ladder of inference" is a useful way to explain how we generate our mental models, our internal maps of external reality. Because we use these mental maps to make sense of our experience and to inform our actions, it's important to get these maps as complete as we can. A shoddy map of reality leads to poor, uninformed choices.

But correcting our ladders is difficult. When we jump up the ladder of inference, it's automatic, skilled behavior, so we often have no conscious awareness of how incomplete and biased our perceptions of reality are. Anyone who's had the experience of "hearing" a friend say "X" when she really means "Y" knows just how easily we race up our ladders in the wrong direction. It's not intentional. Our minds just jump to narrow, error-prone conclusions without our permission, a phenomenon which helps explain this prescient observation made by Joseph Campbell: "There is no way you can use the word 'reality' without quotation marks around it."[7]

This problem is confounded by our default tendency to assume our ladder is correct, and that other people need to correct their erroneous perceptions.[8] Failing to appreciate the degree to which we filter our "reality," we tend to hold our ladders as truth rather than as hypotheses. The cop and the architect, for instance, do not perceive their views as narrow, heavily filtered interpretations of reality but simply as "reality." To the cop, the city *is* a dump. To the architect it *is* beautiful.

This is exactly what happened with the high school students. When they read the cash register story, they went up the ladder in very different directions, completely unaware they were doing it. When they read the statement, "A man appeared after the owner had turned off his store lights," some kids "knew" it was true, while others "knew" it was false. (It's actually unknowable; we don't know if the businessman and the owner are the same person.) Evaluating the statement, "The man who opened the cash register was the owner," most students claimed it was true, some said it was false, and still others deemed it unknowable. (It is unknowable—the story doesn't say whether the owner is a man or woman.) Though the students all read the same four simple sentences, each had a very different interpretation of the story, and they argued over their answers because each student held his or her "ladder" as true.

Ladder of Indifference

Once we've jumped up a ladder and adopted a point of view, it's disturbingly easy to get stuck there. Thanks to a cognitive propensity knows as the *confirmation bias*, once we've reached a conclusion we tend to interpret all subsequent information in a way that reinforces our initial perceptions. "The problem," says Cordelia Fine, "is that we behave like a smart lawyer searching for evidence to bolster his client's case, rather than a jury searching for the truth."[9]

Charles Ornstein of the *Los Angeles Times* shares a sad example of the serious consequences of the confirmation bias when it's poorly managed: "In the emergency room at Martin Luther King, Jr.-Harbor Hospital, Edith Isabel Rodriguez *was seen as a complainer* [italics mine]," he writes. "'Thanks a lot, officers,' an emergency room nurse told Los Angeles County police who brought in Rodriguez. 'This is her third time here.'"[10] Forty-three years old, Edith was the mother of three, and she'd been to the ER three times in three days complaining of pain in her abdomen. She'd been given a prescription and an appointment to see a doctor.

As she arrived this last time, the nurses, having jumped to the conclusion that Rodriguez was just a complainer, admonished her, "You have already been seen, and there is nothing we can do." They left her sitting in a wheelchair in the lobby, where she fell to the floor in excruciating pain for 45 minutes. Assuming she was just putting on an elaborate act, no one came to her aid. A janitor scrubbed the floor around her as she lay writhing on the floor. When Edith's boyfriend showed up on the scene, he raised a ruckus in an attempt to get the hospital staff to help her, but to no avail. Ornstein describes how the incident ended: "Alerted to the 'disturbance' in the lobby, police stepped in—by running Rodriguez's record. They found an outstanding warrant and prepared to take her to jail. She died before she could be put into a squad car."

The staff in the emergency room *assumed* the woman was a "complainer" and then filtered all subsequent events through that label. Even when she fell to the ground in agony, it just bolstered the interpretation that she was an extreme complainer, rather than signaling to these highly trained professionals that it might be a genuine medical emergency. The actual problem, Ornstein reveals, was "a perforated large bowel, which caused an infection. Experts say the condition can bring about death fairly suddenly."

Isabel's sister, Marcela Sanchez, reacted to the news about how her sister died and the disturbing behavior of the ER staff this way: "Where was their heart? Where was their humanity? . . . Everybody was just sitting, looking. Where were they?"

The answer is clear. They were perched high on their erroneous ladders of inference, looking down at the situation with a fatally flawed set of assumptions.

Bong-Hitters and Goose-Steppers

This same problem causes all manner of mischief in business. A few years ago two successful technology companies decided to create a joint venture that would combine and leverage their competitive strengths. They each brought a radically different culture to the endeavor. One firm was renowned for its creative, laid-back, entrepreneurial style, while the other had a buttoned-down, disciplined, process-oriented approach. But as rich as the venture seemed in theory, it wasn't so profitable in practice.

As you might have guessed, it was a ladder problem. People from the rigorous, disciplined organization viewed their "creative" partners, who were usually clad in T-shirts and cargo shorts, as a bunch of "bong-hitting hippies." Conversely, team members from

the creative organization viewed their more disciplined partners—
who showed up for meetings with polished shoes and leather brief-
cases—as "goose-stepping process Nazis." One project member sarcastically commented, "They file into meetings like German troops
marching into Paris."

The hopelessly negative inferences each group was making
about the other made working together a huge problem. The goal
of combining their complementary competencies for competitive
advantage was derailed by their inabilities to manage their ladders
of inference. Rather than look at the abilities of the other group
as an opportunity to build their combined bench strength, each
group adopted a narrow, cynical view of the other, turning a strategic asset into a terminal liability. The joint venture eventually fell
apart, with each group pointing fingers at the other for the failure.
(You can guess which finger the members of the creative group
used.) Lacking the abilities to manage their ladders of inference,
the very differences that made the joint venture valuable ensured
it wouldn't work.

It's a Big Problem

This is the most insidious problem affecting our teams, work relationships, and organizations: *our conflicting ladders of inference and the
minimize and win tendencies we use to manage them.* When J. Edgar
Hoover scribbled, "Watch the borders" on the memo, for example,
he *meant* "Watch the margins on this document." But his team went
up the ladder differently, interpreting the comment as a border se-
curity directive. The biggest problem wasn't the disconnect, it was
the minimize tendencies of his people that kept them from inquiring into the ambiguous comment to clarify what their boss meant.
They compounded a cognitive error with a behavioral one.

The cop and architect story is a metaphor for so many challenging relationships in life: employer and employee, union and business, liberal and conservative, company and customer, marketing and sales, executives and line managers, introvert and extrovert, male and female, engineering and project management. We're all like the cop and the architect, and our natural combination of cognitive limitation and low conversational capacity serves us poorly in all but the simplest of circumstances. It derails projects, sours relationships, escalates misunderstanding, ignites conflict, limits choice, hampers teamwork, and cripples change. And, as we've seen, in extreme circumstances it causes smart, technically astute people to crash their planes and kill their patients. How often do we sit in meetings and watch the cops and architects argue about whose view is *right*—only it's the sales guy and the engineer, or the HR specialist and the operations manager—tripping over their differences in an effort to sell their ladders of inference? We couldn't design a better way to waste our collective brainpower and squander learning.

Poor Ladder Management

Given the imperfect apparatus we're using to make sense of the world, the question isn't whether we'll race up our ladders in limited, self-serving, and erroneous ways—we can't help doing that. It's an inevitable consequence of how our minds work. The only question is how we'll manage our perspectives once we do.

The answer to this question hinges entirely on our conversational capacity. When it's too low, our different "ladders" produce more conflict than learning. If triggered to "win," the cop and the architect argue about whose ladder is "right." If triggered to minimize, on the other hand, the cop and the architect avoid their differences, perhaps by changing the subject. "Well it's certainly lovely weather," the architect comments. "Oh yes, it's a gorgeous day," the cop responds.

No matter which way they move out of the sweet spot, neither the cop nor the architect expands or improves his initial view of the city. Holding on to their tunnel-vision perspectives of "reality" like truths, they stay trapped in their self-sealing interpretive systems, filtering in data that supports their initial inferences and filtering out data that contradicts them. They exist in a perceptual Groundhog Day, reliving the same basic experiences over and over again, repeatedly climbing their same old rickety ladders of inference. There is no pooling of perspectives, no expanded understanding, no "aha" moment. In short, there is no learning.

Effective Ladder Management

It doesn't have to be this way. If the cop and the architect have the discipline to balance candor and curiosity, they treat their ladders like hypotheses rather than truths, transforming their different perspectives into a rich source of learning. As Peter Elbow might put it, the surest way to get hold of what our present ladder binds us to is to adopt the opposite ladder. When we can live with contradiction and exploit it—and explore conflicting ladders—we can simply see and think more.

When their conversational capacity is high, rather than sidestep their differences or squabble over them, they work hard to *explore and understand* them. Once they've each stated their views, "It's a dump" and "It's beautiful," their curiosity kicks in and the inquiry starts.

"You said it was a dump, I thought it was beautiful," the architect might say, "What did you see that I missed?" As he listens to the cop describe what he witnessed walking up the street, the architect's eyes might grow wider as his view of the city expands.

The cop might then inquire by asking, "You said it was beautiful. Obviously I missed something; what did you notice that I didn't?" As the architect describes the aspects of the city on which he focused—buildings, materials, layout, design, history, etc.—the cop might react by saying, "Point a few of those things out to me on the way back to the airport. I'd like to see them."

As they explore the city through their conflicting perspectives—the architect seeing the city through the eyes of the cop, and the cop seeing the city through the eyes of the architect—both men have a more expansive view of the city because they leaned into each other's "ladders." They both expand and improve their mental maps of the city because they're each using more than just their own mind to make sense of it. They increase their collaborative brainpower because they have access to more than just their own biased brain.

We Are All the Cop and the Architect

Again, whenever we talk with other human beings, to one degree or another, we're just like the cop and the architect. We all filter the world around us in distinct, biased, and incomplete ways. If our conversational capacity is high, we know that we each have a unique take on "reality," and we want to get our "ladder" into the conversation as clearly and candidly as possible. But, on the flip side, we also realize we all have our unique blind spots, and if we want to improve our thinking, it's the person who sees things differently we should be working hard to understand.

How do we do this? With our new skillset: by clearly stating our position, explaining our thinking, and then testing it, we put our ladder of inference into the conversation in a clear, intelligent, responsible way. We do this for two reasons: First, we want to allow our unique perspective to influence how others are seeing the issue. We've surely seen things they missed. Second, we're eager to test our ladder, to see what errors and oversights we can detect and correct. In short, we share and test our own ladder. We *inquire* into and *explore* the ladders of others.

This is what the human Flamethrower meant by "push and pull." Before the workshop, he shoved his ladder into a conversation at the expense of those who saw things differently. He never helped pull the ladders of others into meetings or conversations. But once he realized this, he stroved to balance his natural candor with genuine curiosity, putting just as much effort into pulling the thinking of others into conversations as he did into putting his own thoughts forward. He realized that he must sacrifice his need to have his ladder "win" if he wanted to make more informed and effective choices.

In the parent-teacher conference we discussed in Chapter 4, my brother managed the flawed ladder of his student's father by inquiring into it. When the father stated his position, "I'm sick and tired of you giving my daughter bad grades because you don't like the relationship my wife has with this school," he failed to provide any supporting evidence to back up his assertion. But rather than get defensive, my brother got curious, saying, "You've said that I'm giving Julia grades as retribution for your wife's relationship with the school. I'm curious, what signals are you seeing from me that lead you to think that's what's happening here?" When it became clear neither parent could provide any data, my brother shared his ladder of inference about their daughter's grades and tested it with the mother and father. In a textbook example of effective ladder management, Randy worked hard to understand how the parents were making sense of the situation, and just as hard to put forward and test how he was making sense of it.

The key is to lean *our* ladder *into* difference. We don't learn much by engaging people who agree with our views, we learn the most by engaging people who don't. This dramatically increases our ability to detect and correct errors in how we're looking at a situation and to generate a far more accurate mental map. With this in mind, we treat anyone who disagrees with us as the most valuable person in the room. But doing this comes at a cost: it's going to make us less *comfortable* and less *certain*. So if we're committed to improving our mental maps of reality and making more informed and effective choices it's essential we have the discipline to balance candor and courage with curiosity and humility.

Effective Ladder Management and Political Discourse

The power of this discipline for getting people with divergent, strongly held perspectives to work together more effectively was demonstrated in work I conducted with a group of state legislators in the southern United States. In a series of workshops, Republican and Democratic legislators learned the skills and then used them as they grappled with thorny healthcare policy decisions. The results were encouraging.

"We're not nearly as far apart on these issues as I imagined," said one congresswoman after our final session. Each side was able to think less negatively and more expansively because, rather than demonize the view of a colleague, they inquired into it. They weren't seeking agreement—although there was more of that than they expected—but an understanding of the various facets of a complex problem. They were all interested in making the best choices for the people of their states given the tough problems they were facing and the limited resources at their disposal. One participant stated, "Once you sit down together and start looking at the data, a lot of the rhetoric falls away and the choices are much easier to see. Sitting down and really talking was the hard part. The assumptions I was making about some of the people across the aisle were completely wrong."

This was a rare example of productive dialogue in the political arena. It's a shame, because competing ladders can be sources of flexibility and resilience in a pluralistic, multicultural democracy. The United States is known for our highly creative and innovative culture (consider Silicon Valley, our world-renowned institutions of higher education, and our demonstrated ability to bounce back from adversity). Why are we so flexible and creative? A country of immigrants from every corner of the planet, we're the biggest cultural melting pot the world's ever seen. We're a creative and innovative society because we have access to so many different ways of perceiving "reality." A country that can live with contradiction and exploit it—that can use conflicting ladders—can simply see and think more.

But this is true only if the discourse is healthy. It requires, in other words, high conversational capacity—something that is sorely lacking today. Most of our political discourse has devolved into an infantile squabble between the cop and the architect peevishly arguing over who's right and who's wrong.

An Open Mind Is a Smarter Mind

On a bookshelf in my office I have a bumper sticker I purchased from a sidewalk vendor in Berkeley, California, that reads, "Don't believe everything you think." But the more I understand how our minds work, the more I want to scratch out the word *everything* and replace it with *anything*. Given our limited powers of perception, we just can't trust the view of "reality" our minds present to us. As Cordelia Fine aptly puts it, our minds have a mind of their own.

> . . . . *your unscrupulous brain is entirely undeserving of your confidence. It has some shifty habits that leave the truth distorted and*

disguised. Your brain is vainglorious. It's emotional and immoral.
It deludes you. It is pigheaded, secretive, and weak-willed. Oh,
and it's also a bigot. This is more than a minor inconvenience. That
fleshy walnut inside your skull is all you have to know yourself
and to know the world. Yet, thanks to the masquerading of an
untrustworthy brain with a mind of its own, much of what you
know is not quite what it seems. [11]

"Tunnel vision," according to Tom Robbins, "is caused by an optic fungus that multiplies when the brain is less energetic than the ego." [12] If we want to avoid tunnel vision, therefore, our quests to learn must be more energetic than our egos, for a brilliant flash of insight is rarely sparked by someone standing on the same ladder of inference as we are. With this in mind, we should work hard to compensate for the limitations of our minds and treat our opinions, views, and perspectives as suspect—as hypotheses to test rather than truths to protect. We should be more skeptical of our own maps of reality and more curious about the maps of others, not because their maps are any more accurate than our own, but to see what their perspective can teach us about our own map and about the situation we're facing.

This is why low conversational capacity is such a problem: it makes us weak and stupid. It keeps us from learning from our differences, and turns out contrasting points of view into a source of weakness. Cross-functional teams fall apart if they cannot manage their differences effectively. As the bong-hitting hippies and goose-stepping process Nazis clearly demonstrated, if we're unable to balance candor and curiosity, the very differences that could provide tremendous value actually screw us up.

When the going gets tough, as when we're facing change or conflict, or we're forced to navigate unfamiliar territory, it's all the more vital that we have robust conversational capacity, for by turning the cliché that two heads are better than one into an actual practice, it makes us smarter. Don't get me wrong. It's not going to make our brains any bigger, or boost our individual IQs, but it does enable us to see and think more—the essence of being smart—because we're using more than our own heads to make sense of things, a particularly useful thing to do when we're dealing with complex, adaptive challenges. When informed choice is our primary objective, we recognize, to paraphrase Ron Heifetz, that without conflicting ladders of inference, we operate at the mercy of our blind spots, because we cannot prepare for what we do not see.

This matters more than ever. Our world isn't getting more simple and sluggish; it's growing more complex and dynamic. It's increasingly important that we build teams that can deal with the host of arduous, multifaceted problems we're facing, even though we all see them so differently. Lincoln understood this. That's why he pulled into his cabinet men with conflicting political philosophies and agendas. Their divergent perspectives helped him think more expansively and more flexibly about the messy realities he was facing as president. They made him smarter.

It's no different in any team or business, when people with different roles—HR, IT, finance, operations, sales, engineering, and marketing—all have to work together to deal with the complicated challenges they're facing. The mix of functional perspectives, personalities, and agendas is a source of tremendous learning if it's managed well, and a source of crippling dysfunction if it's managed poorly. Conversational capacity, in other words, is the make-or-break competence for building high-learning teams that perform when the pressure is on.

Conversational
Capacity and
Adaptive Learning

The illiterate of the twenty-first century will not be
those who cannot read and write, but those
who cannot learn, unlearn, and relearn.

ALVIN TOFFLER

In the previous chapter we explored how high conversational capacity helps us expand our thinking because we're able to use more than just our own limited, biased maps of reality to make sense of the world. This leads to more informed and effective choices because our access to different ladders of inference allows us to see and think more.

In this chapter we'll see how the capacity to transform conflicting perspectives into learning gives a team an additional advantage that is invaluable in challenging situations where our old ways of thinking no longer fit the bill. People with different perspectives are able to generate not just more learning, but a deeper, more powerful *kind* of learning. They're more agile, astute, and adaptive because they can deliberately *double-loop learn*.[1]

What's with the loops? It has to do with how the concept is explained. To do that, let me share an example that illustrates this kind of learning in action. A few years ago, I facilitated a workshop with a group of 13 CEOs who ran companies of various sizes and from different industries. In the workshop we explored the subject of conversational capacity and practiced the skills as we applied them to the pressing leadership challenges facing the chief executives.

One young CEO led a fast-growing consulting firm with a reputation for stellar service. As the workshop started, he laid out the challenge that was keeping him awake at night. "I have a high-tech consulting business, and we set ourselves apart by hiring people that meet a high standard," he explained. "We have a hard-won reputation for knowledgeable consultants who are easy to work with. So we only hire people with first-rate technical expertise, but we also require them to have great people skills. It's our commitment to finding people with both skills that sets us apart from our competition."

He then explained his problem. "But we're growing rapidly, and I can't find enough of these consultants to keep pace with demand. They're worth their weight in gold and they know it."

"So how have you been dealing with this challenge?" I asked.

"I've been burning through HR directors trying to find one who can help me come up with an effective attraction and retention strategy."

So here's the question: Do you think he's having trouble solving his problem because he needs to read the book *Flawless Execution*[2] and perfect how he's implementing his strategy? Does he need to improve the way he's selecting HR professionals, for example, or sharpen the strategic direction he's providing them once they are hired? Should he try a more rigorous interviewing process to get more reliable information about the true abilities of potential HR directors? Or should he go all the way back to basics and try a new headhunting firm?

I hope you said no to all of these questions, for his problem, as we'll soon see, isn't with how he's *dealing* with the challenge—it's in how he is *making sense* of it.

Not All Learning Is Created Equal

To explain what I mean, let's look at the basic learning process we use as we interact with the world. We *see* a problem ("I can't find enough top-shelf consultants to meet demand"), and then, moving up the ladder of inference, our minds go to work *making sense* of the problem ("I need a savvy HR professional who can help me develop and implement a more effective attraction and retention policy"). Based on how we make sense of the problem, we take *action* ("I've hired a high-priced HR professional who promises he'll fix the problem"). And, finally, our actions produce *consequences* ("We're still not attracting more consultants.")

Whenever there's a gap between the consequences we *intend* and the results we *achieve*, learning is required. There are two very different kinds of learning we can employ. When things don't work out as expected, the easy path is to simply circle back and adjust our actions (our strategy, behavior, or plan). This is called *single-loop learning*.

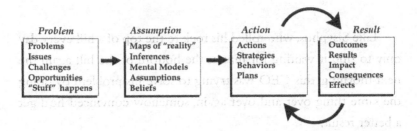

Single-loop learning is fine in routine situations. When our car breaks down, for example, we don't have to *think* too hard about the process by which we approach the problem. But in adaptive circumstances, where the problem is poorly defined, no proven solution exists, and our old habits of thought no longer fit the predicament we're facing, single-loop learning is grossly inadequate. In these situations, if we repeatedly attempt new ways of *dealing* with the problem, we exemplify Albert Einstein's observation that "Insanity is doing the same thing over and over again, expecting a different result."

This was the young CEO's plight. His repeated attempts to hire the right HR professional were not solving the problem, but, without questioning his ladder of inference, he kept at it anyway. When he described how he'd been "burning through HR directors," I could almost hear the squeak of the single-loop hamster wheel on which he was stuck: "I had high hopes for that new HR guy," he seemed to repeatedly think, "but he's not solving the problem. Let's ditch him and try someone else." Single-loop learning by a CEO is charted below.

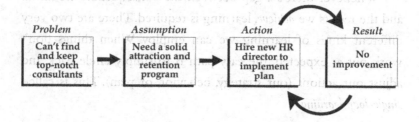

Problem	Assumption	Action	Result
Can't find and keep top-notch consultants	Need a solid attraction and retention program	Hire new HR director to implement plan	No improvement

Like Sisyphus, who rolled his rock to the top of a hill every day only to find it waiting for him at the bottom of the hill again the next morning, this CEO was trying to solve his problem by doing the same thing over and over again, somehow convinced he'd get a better result.

At the end of the workshop, when I asked if anyone had experienced a significant "aha" moment, this young CEO was the first to shoot up his hand. "I did," he said. "I now realize that the very people I'm trying to attract to my business *will not work for someone like me.*" This was a momentous shift in his understanding of the challenge he was facing. He was no longer concentrating on how to *address* the problem; he was focused instead on how he was *framing* it.

"Would you be willing to explain that 'aha' in more detail?" I asked.

"Sure. I grew this business from the ground up, and I have strong ideas about how things should be done. I've got an intense need to win, so someone with a different idea doesn't get far with me. Why would a top consultant—the kind of person we're trying to hire—want to work someplace where they're not listened to and their ideas aren't valued?" He immediately answered his own question: "Fact is, they don't. And I think that's why we're having such a hard time landing the right people. And to make things worse, I've surrounded myself with a team that acts just as I do. So I've done a great job of creating a culture that's repelling the very people we're trying to attract.

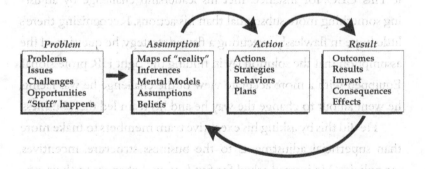

This tectonic shift in the CEO's thinking wasn't painless. It didn't make him feel comfortable or right, but it did help him make far more informed decisions about how to lead and grow his business.

Armed with this new insight, he and his team buckled down and did the hard work of changing how he and his executives interacted with, and learned from, their high-powered consultants. By learning to balance candor and curiosity, they systematically increased the conversational capacity of their entire company, cultivating an environment that attracted the kind of people they needed to grow the business. Every person in his organization is now trained in the discipline, which they use to manage their internal teamwork as well as their consulting relationships with clients. What was the result? The company has more than doubled in size, and it's been rated "the best place to work" by its home city for several years in a row.

Hopping Off the Hamster Wheel

When we double-loop learn we hop off our hamster wheel of thought and question the way we've made sense of the problem in the first place. The more complex and unfamiliar the challenge we're facing, the more important it becomes to test and adjust the underlying ladders of inference, beliefs, and filters we're using to tackle it. This CEO, for instance, met his leadership challenge by adjusting something more substantial than his actions. Recognizing there's little hope in flawlessly executing a flawed strategy, he questioned the assumption that the solution lay in finding the right HR professional. Equipped with a more accurate view of the challenge he was facing, he went all out to change the way he and his team led their business.

He did this by asking his executive team members to make more than superficial adjustments to the business structure, incentives, or policies. He instead asked for fundamental changes to their attitudes and beliefs about leadership, their operating values, their ways of framing the business and their roles in it. He and his team pulled together and *double-loop learned*.

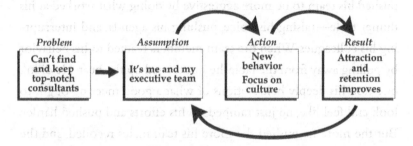

Double-Loop Dialogue

This transformational shift in the CEO's thinking didn't occur by listening to people who agreed with his current strategy. It happened because he leaned into the views of people who didn't. His "ruthlessly compassionate"[3] partners in his CEO peer group helped him confront the unwelcome reality that his own behavior—and that of his executive team—was the primary source of his trouble.

"If you're open to feedback, I'll take a stab at it. I'm kind of surprised you think it's an HR issue," one of his colleagues opened up. "I've known you for years, and I think you are the problem. I'm not saying this to be callous, so let me tell you what I mean, and then you can tell me off if you think I'm full of it." It was by opening himself to the contrasting "ladders" of his colleagues that he was able to see his predicament in a radically different way.

"I'm All Push, No Pull"

The human Flamethrower underwent a similar double-loop shift in consciousness. His view of a good meeting included lots of arguing, intense debate, and many people talking at once. To his way of thinking, argumentative, combative discussions were a sign that things were going well. Based on this deep-seated assumption, he pushed his team to be more aggressive by doing what worked at his dinner table—raising his voice, pushing his agenda, and interrupting his colleagues. When the team members reacted to his behavior by pulling away from the table, he just turned up the heat. He didn't question his deeply held notions of what a good meeting ought to look and feel like, he just ramped up his efforts and pushed harder. But the more he pushed the more his teammates recoiled, and the more they recoiled the harder he pushed. The entire team was running itself ragged on a single-loop hamster wheel.

They were all smart people. They all wanted to be part of a highly effective team, yet around and around they went, blind to how they were all contributing to their team's downward spiral of dysfunction. Their good intentions were no match for their inability to transform their conflicting ideas about teamwork into double-loop learning.

All that changed when the Flamethrower had his double-loop "aha" moment. Recognizing his programmed behavior was "all push, no pull," he put tremendous energy into changing how he worked with his colleagues. Like the young CEO, the pivotal shift wasn't in his actions; it was in his assumptions and beliefs about what constitutes effective teamwork.

Single-Loop Smart but Double-Loop Dumb

The capacity for double-loop learning is not the product of intellectual firepower. It's the result of high conversational capacity. When their capacity is low, even extremely intelligent, highly committed people can get trapped in their flawed maps of "reality."

NASA offers a case in point. Early on the morning of February 2, 2003, as the space shuttle *Columbia* was reentering the earth's atmosphere, a few lower-level engineers at NASA were worried about foam. Just over two weeks prior, Columbia had launched into orbit. It was the 113th shuttle launch for NASA, and the 28th launch for *Columbia*. At launch, the shuttle is attached to powerful solid rocket boosters each covered with orange insulating foam. "Eighty-two seconds after liftoff, as the *Columbia* was accelerating through at 1,500 mph, a piece of that foam—about 19 inches long by 11 inches wide, weighing about 1.7 pounds—broke off the external tank and collided with the left wing at about 545 mph," writes William Langewiesche, author of the article *"Columbia's* Last Flight," a lucid account of the accident and its underlying causes.[4]

After reviewing a film of the launch, engineers were concerned about the foam strike, which appeared to hit a sensitive area at the leading edge of the wing. But the engineers minimized and covered up their concern because it contradicted a hallowed belief of NASA management: "It had become a *matter of faith* within NASA that foam strikes—which were a known problem—could not cause mortal damage to the shuttle."[5] It's now obvious that the concerns of the engineers were justified, for a short while after the shuttle reentered the earth's atmosphere, *"Columbia* lay scattered for 300 miles across the ground."[6]

When the investigation into the cause of the accident commenced, engineers immediately suspected the foam strike. But management, holding tight to their beliefs that a foam strike couldn't be the source of the problem, reacted defensively to their concerns. They remained "stubbornly closed-minded on the subject of foam," says Langewiesche. NASA management not only refused to explore the possibility that the foam strike caused the fatal damage, in a disturbing display of win behaviors they openly ridiculed the engineers who put forward the suggestion, publicly dismissing them as "foamologists."

Just like the cop and the architect, engineers and management at NASA went up divergent ladders of inference. When engineers looked at the foam strike, they immediately thought, "This is a big deal. We should investigate this." When management looked at it, their response was, in essence, "This isn't a big deal. Don't worry about it." Rather than get curious and explore the perspective of the engineers, managers protected their own single-loop assumptions by belittling the engineers and dismissing their concerns.

The engineers weren't the only group to experience NASA management's chronic lack of curiosity. The Columbia Accident Investigation Board (CAIB) asked NASA to conduct a test that involved firing a chunk of foam at the leading edge of a spare orbiter wing. The experiment was designed to test the engineers' hypothesis that the foam strike caused the shuttle to disintegrate by allowing superheated atmospheric gases to penetrate the wing on reentry. But since it was the last spare wing, and they "knew" the foam wasn't the cause, management stubbornly resisted the experiment.

Frustrated, CAIB took over the test and conducted it in front a large crowd, including some of the very people who had complained the test was a waste of time. The test involved several shots in which pieces of foam were fired at the wing at graduated speeds. When the first shot caused no significant damage, some managers—still clinging to their hamster-wheel assumptions that foam strikes posed no mortal risk—mocked the results.

But it was the last shot that most closely replicated the strike the engineers believed had actually occurred. Langewiesche describes the scene: "The gun fired, and the foam hit the panel at a 25-degree relative angle at about 500 mph. Immediately afterward an audible gasp went through the crowd. The foam had knocked a hole in the [wing] large enough to allow people to put their heads through." Some in attendance were so taken aback they broke into tears. The test had not only blown a large hole in the leading edge of the wing; it blew an even larger hole in NASA management's assumptions about the danger of foam strikes.

The destructive combination of a top-down culture, technical complexity, entrenched bureaucracy, and low conversational capacity trapped NASA management on a single-loop hamster wheel in the very circumstances in which they most needed to double-loop learn. Management was arrogantly attached to their tired old thinking, holding their assumption about foam strikes as an absolute truth to be accepted rather than a hypothesis to be tested. What would have happened had they shown more curiosity and questioned that assumption before the shuttle began reentry? We'll never know.

And, the other side of the coin, what if the engineers, like Dr. Pronovost in the first chapter, had spoken up and said, "We think this foam strike warrants further investigation. If we're wrong, it's no big deal. But if you're wrong, you could destroy the shuttle and kill the astronauts. So we'd strongly suggest taking a closer look at the possibility that this foam strike is different from all the others we've seen in the past. What's your reaction to this way of looking at the situation?" Again, we'll never know.

As we've seen again and again, the problem wasn't technical, it was social. These were smart people. They had good intentions. But their unwillingness to question their basic assumptions—a hallmark of the rigorous scientific and engineering mindset—signaled a pattern of sloppy thinking that runs counter to the very mission of NASA. Like the kids in the classroom, managers jumped to unverified conclusions, treated those conclusions as sacred truths, and maligned anyone calling them into question. This closed-minded approach led to uninformed decisions because they weren't willing to explore the conflicting perspectives of their engineers. More cocky than curious, they were single-loop smart but double-loop dumb.

It's a Common Problem

Day to day the impact of low conversational capacity and single-loop learning may not be so extreme, but it is an extremely common problem. In one of my workshops, Harry, a manager of a large construction firm in Toronto, described to his fellow workshop participants the loud and combative arguments he and his team had in meetings. They were, as he put it, "very intense." He said that their meeting room was in the middle of the office, so that when they fought, everyone could hear it. This created a problem because the meetings were so loud and aggressive that people around the office became increasingly reticent to deal with the managers for fear of having the same behavior directed at them. "It was a big problem," Harry said. Another participant in the workshop then asked, "So what did you do about it?"

"It was easy. We're a construction firm. We just double-insulated the meeting room," Harry answered.

"I think you're on a hamster wheel!" said another participant.

Thanks to our confirmation bias, every day people get stuck with single-loop interpretations *of each other*. If I see my colleague Bob as difficult, I often interpret all my future interactions with Bob through this filter. I pay attention to behaviors that confirm my initial view and ignore data that suggests it may be inaccurate. Once I've created a filter for Bob, it can be very hard for Bob to get off the ladder on which I've placed him, and just as hard for me to question it and double-loop learn.

"Evidence that fits with our beliefs is quickly waved through the mental border control," explains Cordelia Fine. "Counter-evidence, on the other hand, must submit to close interrogation and even then will probably not be allowed in. As a result, people can wind up holding their beliefs even more strongly after seeing counterevidence. It's as if we think, 'Well, if *that's* the best that the other side can come up with then I really must be right.' This phenomenon, called belief polarization, may help to explain why attempting to disillusion people of their perverse misconceptions is often futile."[7]

This is precisely what happened as Edith Isabel Rodriguez writhed in pain on the floor of the emergency room at Martin Luther King, Jr.-Harbor Hospital. The staff assumed she was just a "complainer" and kept interpreting her escalating signs of trouble as additional proof. Sadly, it was only after she died that they recognized their fatally flawed assumption.

Simple in Theory but Hard in Practice

Double-loop learning is the process of surfacing, questioning, improving, and changing our ladder of inference, and the habitual ways we go up it, so we can make better, more effective choices. Like a group of skilled jazz musicians, a team that can deliberately double-loop learn is more nimble and adaptable in the face of unusual, shifting, complex circumstances because team members can better adjust their thinking to fit the new challenge.

But there's a catch. Much like the conversational capacity skills that promote it, this kind of learning is extraordinarily difficult to orchestrate because people and their teams tend to be *allergic* to it. For one thing, having our favored perspective invalidated is not likely to feel reassuring, and, at least in the short term, it's unlikely to make us feel brilliant. So to double-loop learn, our willingness to improve our thinking must be greater than our need to feel comfortable or right. But it's not just our primal fight-or-flight tendencies that make double-loop learning such a daunting challenge. Four other obstacles also stand in our way:

➤ Blindness

➤ Attachment

➤ Resistance

➤ Uncertainty

Blindness

For starters, we often look right through our assumptions without even realizing how they're affecting our perceptions. As Tom Robbins bluntly puts it, "the difference between us and Helen Keller is that she knew she was deaf and blind." [8] Undetected, our assumptions serve as invisible filters shaping how we perceive "reality" yet we're blind to their presence. This presents a major barrier to double-loop learning because we can't question, improve, or change an assumption we can't see.

The Flamethrower held an assumption that being *right* is the same as being *effective*, but for years he took no responsibility for this interpretation of reality because he was unaware he was holding it. He never questioned the assumption—which led to the feisty, aggressive behavior that was pushing away his teammates—because it was the product of his upbringing, something he'd acquired unconsciously by absorbing the conversational norms in his family. He was, in effect, completely *blind* to it. But when his mental model about conversation was finally illuminated so he could see it clearly, the Flamethrower immediately recognized its folly. "That's my problem. I am all push, no pull," he declared, and went to work intentionally changing his operating mindset.

Attachment

The second barrier to double-loop learning is that we're often overly *attached* to our thinking, and it's hard to correct something we're unwilling to change. We behave like the prisoners of war in the classic film *Bridge on the River Kwai*,[9] in which a group of British prisoners are forced by their captors to build a bridge over the aforementioned river. It's a tricky engineering challenge, materials are wanting, and they endure brutal treatment by their captors, but despite these obstacles they rise to the challenge and build an elegant wooden bridge spanning the river.

Allied commandos eventually sneak in, provide the prisoners with a satchel of explosives, and tell them to blow up the bridge. Strategically, it's the right thing to do, but a funny thing happens—the prisoners don't want to blow it up. They've put a lot work into that bridge. It's pulled them together as a team. It's a reflection of the courage, pride, and tenacity of the British spirit; so, even though it's the right thing to do, they can't bring themselves to destroy it. They've grown *attached* to their bridge.

We often treat our own thinking like the bridge on the river Kwai. We've put a lot of work into our mental models, and they've worked well in the past, so even when they're no longer serving us well—as with NASA management and their assumptions about foam strikes—we resist blowing them up. "Our big assumptions are like favorite hypotheses, and we are like the sort of scientists who, should they meet disconfirming data, say in effect, 'Well, so much the worse for the data!' Out it goes, and the precious hypothesis is preserved," say Robert Kegan and Lisa Laskow Lahey.[10] Our minds, in other words, have a self-serving, single-loop tendency to resist information that threatens our current view of reality, so they filter the world around us so we see what we want to see. And what do we *want* to see? Anything that tells us we're on the right hamster wheel; anything that saves us from having to blow up our bridge.

Resistance

The third reason this kind of learning is so challenging is that defenders of the status quo often persecute a person who advocates a double-loop perspective. When we muster the courage to raise our hand and suggest a double-loop point of view, we're often treated like Galileo, who was labeled a heretic and put under house arrest by the Inquisition for championing the Copernican model of our place in the cosmos—an accurate double-loop shift that places the Sun, not Earth, at the center of our solar system.

When people, teams, and organizations react *defensively* to an idea, what is it they're *defending*? Their current idea and the assumptions, beliefs, and mental models on which it stands—the very things they need to question and adjust in order to double-loop learn. NASA management defended their sacred assumption about foam strikes, for example, by publicly ridiculing the engineers as "foamologists." Rather than open their minds and explore an idea that contradicted their current view (perhaps a foam strike can produce a mortal problem for the shuttle), they chose to protect their fatally flawed perspective. Publicly branded "foamalogists" for merely doing their jobs, the engineers were "Galileo-ed" for questioning the religious orthodoxy about foam strikes.

Uncertainty

Yet another reason we're allergic to double-loop learning is that it provokes tremendous uncertainty. It's one thing to know our current way of framing the problem *isn't* working; it's another thing to know which way of framing it *will*. Blowing up our mental bridge on the river Kwai necessitates constructing a more useful one, a process that requires people with different views of the problem— the cops and the architects—to start learning from one another to figure out a more effective way forward.

But getting people with conflicting views to learn from one another takes us right back to our fundamental problem—the visceral fight-or-flight reactions that make learning from contrarian perspectives so difficult. In order to deliberately double-loop learn, our conversational capacity needs be more robust than our need to defend our point of view. It's easier to blow up our current mental "bridge" if we're confident we can work with others to construct a better one. But to enjoy this confidence we must undergo our own Copernican revolution, replacing our egos with informed choices at the center of our conversations.

Proactive Double-Loop Learning

When it comes to double-loop learning, we have three options: double-loop *proactively*, double-loop *reactively*, or don't double-loop at all. When the CEO realized his own behavior, and not his HR policy, was restricting his company's growth, he proactively changed how he was framing the challenge. He didn't wait until after his business tanked before making the double-loop shift.

NASA management's double-loop "aha," by contrast, was reactive. Yes, they eventually adjusted their assumptions that a foam strike couldn't pose a mortal risk to the shuttle, but even the destruction of the *Columbia* and the death of its crew didn't provide sufficient catalyst for the shift. It was only after the Columbia Accident Investigation Board blew a hole in the leading edge of the spare wing that they realized the test had also blown apart their sacred theory about foam strikes.

Some teams and organizations never get off their hamster wheels. If they're routinely getting the results they desire, this is okay—no need to reinvent the wheel if it's producing what we want it to. But some teams—like the groups from two culturally different companies in Silicon Valley we met in the last chapter— remain trapped on the hamster wheel of single-loop learning simply because they lack the capacity to hop off.

Obviously, proactive double-loop learning is the preferable option, and getting people with differing and conflicting views to lean into their differences is essential. "If people don't engage across the divide of their differences, there is no learning," says Ron Heifetz. "People don't learn by looking in the mirror. They learn by talking with people who have different points of view."[11] If we want to unlock the door to proactive double-loop learning, conversational capacity provides the key.

At its best, Vistage, an organization of peer advisory groups for over 15,000 CEOs around the world, strives to facilitate proactive double-loop learning. It does this by putting together groups ranging from 12 to 16 CEOs running a wide variety of businesses, from large to small and from different industries. These groups meet every month for a full day, and executives bring their opportunities, problems, and decisions to meetings to have their thinking questioned, vetted, and refined in the crucible of feedback from their fellow CEOs. They don't do this because it's painless and fun. They do it to improve and expand how they're thinking about their biggest challenges. When a CEO drives home from a Vistage meeting after sharing a problem with her colleagues, she's in a position to make a far more informed and effective choice because she's been exposed to a range of differing views, data, and perspectives. Much like Lincoln and his team of rivals, Vistage has figured out that the best way to facilitate a profound shift in our effectiveness is to lean into difference, not because it's easy, but because it sparks the most profound learning.

Working in the Sweet Spot Requires Double-Loop Learning

Because conflict is the primary catalyst for double-loop learning, only teams with reliably high conversational capacity can deliberately orchestrate it. When it's lacking we're rendered impervious to proactive double-loop learning because the contrasting perspectives that would help us hop off our hamster wheel instead trigger our fight-or-flight responses. When we're hooked by these base tendencies, we circle our defensive wagons to protect the very thing that needs adjustment—our inferences, assumptions, values, and beliefs.

This presents us with another catch-22: double-loop learning is dependent on high conversational capacity, but building our conversational capacity entails double-loop learning; it requires a major shift in our mindset, not just a simple change in our actions. But this quandary isn't unusual. We face the same basic problem when learning any new skill. Remember the HR professional who flinched when he first put forward and tested his view, afraid that someone might actually push back on his thinking. With ongoing practice he eventually reached a point where he was *disappointed* when no one disagreed with him. In a similar way, to build our own conversational capacity, we must develop an adoptive loop, where the more we use the skills, the more we develop the mindset, and the more we develop the mindset, the more we use the skills. (In Chapter 8 we'll explore strategies for creating just such a double-loop learning process.)

An Essential Competence

Holding our ideas, views, and perspectives more like hypotheses that need to be tested—a hallmark characteristic of a more disciplined mindset—is conducive to double-loop learning. When we hold a view like truth it makes it much harder to question it, much less correct it. But when we treat our thoughts, assumptions, and beliefs as suspect, it makes it easier to adjust or change them when they don't pass muster. This is a more mindful and humble way of managing our thoughts. By candidly and courageously sharing *our* ladders and then humbly and curiously comparing them with *the ladders of others*, we're treating our perspectives as simple tools for making sense of the world around us rather than sacred truths we'll be damned for changing.

Given the rapidly evolving world in which we live, people and teams who can orchestrate double-loop learning are increasingly vital because the number of novel, complicated, wicked challenges we face is rapidly mounting. If we don't strengthen our ability to learn and adapt in dynamic circumstances, we'll begin the slide, as my colleague Benjamin Akande puts it, to increasing irrelevance. Left unchecked, our inability to learn, grow, and change leads to what he refers to as team and organizational "hospice."[12]

If insanity is doing the same thing over and over again expecting a different result, then low conversational capacity leads to insane teams. Trapped on the hamster wheel of their outdated thinking, unable to adapt to the novel predicaments they face, a team that can't deliberate double-loop learn grows increasingly ineffective in a dynamic environment. The team demonstrates that insanity is *thinking* the same thing over and over again, expecting a different result.

The Work of Building a Disciplined Team

....

Good ideas are not adopted automatically.
They must be driven into practice with
courageous patience.

HYMAN RICKOVER

hen it comes to skill, it's not what we know that counts, but what we can put into practice. It's not uncommon for someone to say, "I know that to be more effective I must balance my win tendency with higher curiosity and humility," and yet five minutes later that same person is berating a colleague who dared to disagree. So if we want to build our conversational capacity, how do we move beyond mere awareness toward real competence?

Unlike Neo in *The Matrix*, there is no red pill we can take to facilitate this transformative shift in our mindset, no computer into which we can be plugged to effortlessly download the skills. As with any genuine discipline, be it playing the piano or earning a black belt in karate, both practice and instruction are required. Fortunately, our daily experience at work provides the first, and this book and the people with whom you read and discuss it can serve as the second.

When we subordinate our habitual need to minimize or win in the service of informed choice, we're changing the governing norms by which we participate in meetings, conversations, and decisions. It's a double-loop venture, requiring not just a superficial tweak to our behavior but a deep shift in what we *value* in a conversation. But learning to set aside these tendencies and balance candor and curiosity is a frustrating endeavor, rife with slipups and setbacks. This is to be expected. Frustration is an integral part of any skill-building process. We'd laugh at someone who said, "I don't like being frustrated, so I'm not going to practice the piano until I'm good at it." That's why it's called *practice*—it *implies* slipups and setbacks.

Changing Our Brains

The neuroplasticity research of Jeffrey Schwartz and his colleagues at UCLA shows that by learning to recognize when a tendency is being triggered, and then practicing replacement behaviors, people can more mindfully manage even extreme behavioral reactions such as those associated with Tourette's syndrome and obsessive-compulsive disorder (OCD).[1] Their research demonstrates that as people consistently practice the replacement behaviors, they actually change the physical structure of their brains, because, just like a muscle, the neural circuits for any activity grow where they're being used and atrophy where they're being neglected. Our brains, in other words, get stronger when they're being exercised. These changes are demonstrable. As we practice any new discipline, whether it's playing the violin or driving a car, the growth in regions of the brain associated with the new skills can be tracked and measured with functional magnetic resonance imaging.[2]

This is encouraging news. If it's possible to recognize and manage the powerful reactions associated with Tourette's syndrome and

OCD, we can certainly do the same with our habitual minimize and win responses. As we practice conversing in the sweet spot day by day, we literally weaken the power of our old habits as we strengthen our capacity with new ones. With regular practice, we produce a flywheel effect, where the more we use the skills, the more our skills grow, and the more our skills grow, the more we use the skills.

Is it hard work? Sure it is. Any skill worth learning takes effort. But if we put as much time and effort into building our capacity to remain in the sweet spot as we did learning to perfect our golf swing, master a yoga pose, or beat a video game, we'd be very different people leading very different lives. We'd literally change our brains and live lives more and more guided by our better angels and less and less by our primal impulses.

Two Kinds of Work: Personal Work and Teamwork

When it comes to practice, there's good news—the workplace is a rich source of opportunities. "Problems," the actor John Cusack once said, "are the instruments of [our] evolution,"[3] and if there is one thing our workplaces aren't lacking, it's problems. Chock full of decisions, difficult people, contrasting perspectives, relentless change, and time-pressured goals, the workplace is the ultimate dojo for building our conversational capacity. Viewed this way, our daily work experience is transformed into a vehicle for building our discipline, with every decision and meeting a chance for experimentation and learning. Things we previously considered merely bothersome—a stressful project, difficult colleague, demanding boss, or dysfunctional meeting—become useful opportunities to practice and learn.

This is a big deal. We spend a large chunk of our lives in our vocational dojo, and we can spend that time becoming more aware of the issues, situations, people, and behaviors that trigger us to minimize or win, and then treat those factors as golden opportunities for practicing our skills. In situations where we tend to minimize, strengthening our facility with the candor skills is the best way to balance out our natural style. In situations that trigger our need to win, learning to respond with more curiosity and humility provides the most value.

Learning to recognize how mindlessly our behaviors and our intentions part ways is the first step, because we're often oblivious to the disconnect. In a workshop with several top managers, for instance, after I described the four skills and their ability to help us balance candor and curiosity, one feisty manager blurted out, "That's just common sense. I can't believe you're making a big deal about all this. I already do that."

"No, you don't," I replied, using this manager's derogatory reaction to make a point.

"Yes, I do," shot back the manager.

"No, you don't."

"*Yes, I do!*" he fired back, raising his voice and sticking to his guns.

Overriding my urge to minimize, I again repeated my position, "No, you obviously don't."

"Fuck you, asshole!" he exploded. "You don't even know me."

The class erupted in laughter. As he looked around at his fellow managers, he began to laugh too, slowly realizing what had happened.

If you were watching from the sidelines, the entire episode was comical. I was suggesting that when someone puts forward a strong position but fails to explain it, it's useful to inquire into his or her unexplained position—not to agree with it, but to understand it, to see what it can teach us about our own perspective. This manager argued that this was "common sense," boldly declaring, "I already do that." But when I immediately pushed back with a position, "No, you don't," rather than inquire into it, he argued back—an egregious violation of the "commonsense" behavior he claimed he used. And until the group's laughter highlighted what was happening, he was completely blind to the gap between his espoused "commonsense" behavior and his actual triggered behavior.[4]

It's a problem to which we're all prone. So how do we close the gap between our intentions and our behavior? What does the practice entail? To use the workplace as a gymnasium for increasing both our awareness and our skill, we focus on two kinds of work: *personal work* and *teamwork.*

Personal Work

A disciplined team is made up of disciplined team members. We have no hope of helping our team communicate in the sweet spot if we lack the capacity to stay there ourselves. Personal work, therefore, is the work required to bring more balance to our own minimize and win inclinations. With this in mind, let's review a variety of activities for building our capacity to remain open, balanced, and nondefensive under stress.

Meeting time is practice time. Use every meeting, problem, decision, conflict, or change as an opportunity to build your skills. There should be no such thing as a boring meeting because you're practicing as you participate, facilitate, or both. If you care about an issue, manage the conversations with as much discipline as possible. If you're not interested in the subject matter, practice your skills by helping those people who do care engage the topic in a balanced and productive way. Either way, by "listening to what's being played and then playing what's missing," you're using every meeting to push the boundaries of your conversational competence.

Become a reflective practitioner. "We know the world through our relationship to it," observed M. Scott Peck. "Therefore, to know the world, we must not only examine it but we must examine the examiner."[5] Keeping this in mind, get curious about your emotional and conversational balance. Constantly ask questions such as, "Am I being both candid and curious? If not, what can I do to be more balanced?" Pay close attention to your reactions. What threw you off center? Was it a colleague's conflicting view, or the colleague's snarky tone of voice? Did he or she seem arrogant or dismissive when putting forward an idea? When you experience this behavior again, what would be a healthier, more disciplined response? What would bring more balance to how you participate in the team? Remember, every time you lose balance, it's another opportunity to learn about your emotional hotspots and knee-jerk responses. As you become more conscious of your own reactions, and the situations under which they hook you, you'll be better able to make more mindful choices about how to act in the moment.

Look in the mirror. When first learning this discipline, one danger is the tendency to use the new frameworks to judge everyone else's behavior rather than focus on your own. "She's not testing her views," you might think to yourself, or, "Unbelievable. He's just trying to win the conversation and get his way." This external focus is predictable because it's easy and pain-free. Taking a hard look at the gap between your own intentions and behavior—and then doing something about it—is far more challenging work. Your naturally self-serving tendency to look outward, in other words, is a defensive routine: You avoid looking at your own behavior by placing all your attention on the behavior of others.

Adopting such a judgmental attitude is an exercise in arrogance, while taking a hard look in the mirror is an exercise in humility. To avoid the arrogance trap, you should be constantly asking yourself reflective questions: "What are my intentions in this conversation or meeting? Do I need to refocus on informed choice? Have I drifted off to min or win? If so, what would bring me back into balance?"

Focus on one skill at a time. If you have a strong win tendency, for instance, practice testing your views for a couple of weeks. Once that skill becomes a more natural part of your behavioral repertoire, put your emphasis on the skill of inquiry. In a few short weeks, you can make a demonstrable shift in your conversational capacity by breaking the discipline down into bite-sized chunks of practice and learning.

Adopt a learner's mindset. Be open-minded and curious even when you blow it. When you notice you've dropped the ball, celebrate the fact that you noticed, and then pick up the ball and try again. Be more curious than critical, even with your own behavior. When you slide out of the sweet spot, respond by thinking, "How interesting," as opposed to, "I'm such a screw-up."

Document your progress. Keep a trigger journal, and track the issues and circumstances that trigger your min or win reactions. One CEO, blessed with an abundance of candor, desperately wanted to bring more curiosity to his behavior but found he had a hard time recognizing the moment he snapped into win mode. I asked him to keep a trigger journal. Every day at lunch, and at the end of the day before heading home, he'd make note of any situation where he "lost discipline" and left the sweet spot. "What was the triggering event?" he'd note, "What was my reaction? What would have been a healthier, more balanced response?" Over time his journal entries changed, demonstrating his progress. More and more his entries started to read like this: "What was the triggering event? What was my balanced response? What would have been my old, habitual reaction?"

Seek regular feedback. Ask team members, friends, or colleagues about your tendencies and how well you're managing them.

"What about my behavior makes it hard for other people to stay in the sweet spot? What are my tendencies, and how are they displayed?" Periodic feedback can be one of the most powerful (if not always the most comfortable) ways of making the shift from ego-centered to intention-centered behavior. You might ask a friend or colleague to monitor your behavior and report back to you. "How am I doing? Provide me feedback at the end of each meeting, or at the end of each week, as to how I am doing with my balance. Keep an eye on me during the meeting and let me know how I'm doing during the breaks. I'd be happy to return the favor if you'd like."

Enroll your teammates. Beyond mere feedback, jointly enroll other people to help you stay focused on the behaviors you want to change. "I am working on testing for the next two weeks, and, if you're willing, I'd like your help. If you see me forget to test in a meeting, I ask that you jump in and test for me." Or, "If you see me put forward a position but fail to share my thinking, please nudge me along by inquiring into my point." Or, "I'll need support if I'm going to improve. When you see me slipping back to my old win behaviors, let's agree on a signal."

Study. Work to understand the key ideas you're trying to learn. Read this book more than once. Read other articles or research. Make sure you have more than just a superficial awareness and that you understand what you're up against.

Teach it to others. Explain the concepts and skills to family and friends. Get them thinking about key ideas such as conversational capacity, the sweet spot, minimizing and winning, and the behaviors that balance push and pull.

Be patient. You're not going to be a master right away. Gradually expanding the boundaries of your competence requires focus, consistency, and determination.

Mindfulness practice. Since deliberately balancing candor and curiosity requires that you communicate more mindfully, activities such as meditation, yoga, or meditative running, which strengthen our awareness, are powerful ways to increase your competence. My recommendation is this: If you don't have a regular mindfulness practice, start one. If you do have one, keep it up. "Mindful Awareness Practices," or MAPS[6] as they're called (putting a new spin on the term "mental MAPS"), help sharpen your capacity for self-awareness. And since you can't manage a reflex if you're unaware of it, developing a part of your mind that is able to watch your behavior *in the moment* is essential.

Mindfulness practice does just this. It cultivates your "observer self," that part of your mind that pays attention to how your mind is working. This is a vital competence in difficult circumstances. When one part of your mind is busy on the dance floor of thought—thinking, analyzing, reacting, drifting, and so on—another part of your mind is watching it do so from a mental balcony. The more you're able to get up on the balcony and observe your reactions on the dance floor, the more informed will be the choices at your disposal for mindfully managing those reactions.

Imagine two people sitting in a meeting in which their needs to minimize is triggered. One has a well-developed observer self and is able to recognize the reaction and take appropriate action. "I feel the need to keep my mouth shut and play it safe, but I am going to override that reaction and raise my hand." The other person, lacking that mindfulness, just shuts down, unaware that he or she is even doing so.

Mindfulness is not a religious ritual, it's a practice, a mental exercise; and like running, it takes a lot of effort and patience to master. To go long distances in running, we have to gradually increase our strength and endurance. In a very similar way, becoming reliably mindful in our interactions with others requires ongoing dedication, practice, and patience. It's surprisingly challenging at first. But with consistent practice you can increase the amount of time you're able to remain on your mental balcony—less closed-minded and reactive and more open-minded and curious.

This mental discipline allows us a greater level of control over our behavior because our "observer self" is more developed, allowing us to make more informed choices about how to respond to a given situation because we're more aware of our tendencies and better able to rein them in when necessary. An executive I know prides himself on his skill at controlling his Porsche at high speed on a challenging track. By increasing his mindfulness he can bring just as much skill to how he manages his own mental state, to keeping his emotional reactions on track, and to maintain his ability to align his behavior and his intentions under pressure.

It's not hocus-pocus. The positive impact mindfulness has on performance is so well documented that doctors are now being trained to meditate to improve their capacity to work in an increasingly complex, fast-paced, and high-stakes environment.[7] Research demonstrates that doctors who had some sort of mindfulness practice become more "present, attentive and focused on the moment and less emotionally exhausted over time. Moreover, the doctors' ability to empathize with patients and understand how patients' families and work lives or social situations could influence their illnesses increased and persisted even after the course had ended." Dr. Ronald Epstein, a professor of family medicine, psychiatry, and oncology at the University of Rochester Medical Center who developed a course in mindfulness for doctors, argues that "mindfulness awareness practice, and the self-awareness it cultivates, is a fundamental ingredient of excellent care."[8]

Use partners. Use partners to prepare for important conversations. If the conversation is a 10 on the difficulty scale, but your current skill level tops out at about 7, you need to bridge the gap. Sitting down with colleagues and having them help you think through what you need to say, and how to say it, is supremely helpful. What is your position? How can you explain it and test it? What reactions might the other person have, and how can you inquire to better understand them? Use role-play to test your ability to put into practice the balanced approach you've designed. In my workshops, I regularly see people whittle 5 or 6 points off the self-reported difficulty of a conversation after an hour of such practice.

Give notice. Alert people ahead of time of an upcoming conversation so they have time to prepare and practice. By way of agenda or e-mail, for example, explain your position and your thinking, and end it with a test: "If you have a different view on this, let's get together and discuss it. I'd like to explore how you're looking at this issue."

Record a meeting and "score" your balance. Listen to a recording of your participation in a meeting or conversation and score your use of the skills. How do you rate? Lots of candor but not as much curiosity? Are you putting forward clear positions? How well do you articulate your thinking? Do you test your views? Was your test as strong as or stronger than the position you put forward? How about inquiry? Did you help pull the views of others into the dialogue? (If you decide to record yourself, make sure to get permission to record first, and to explain why you're doing it.)

Be the productive variable. "There is no contact between human beings that does not affect both of them," said Erich Fromm.[9] From a systems perspective, by improving just one variable in a system, the whole system is affected. So when you roll up your sleeves and improve your own conversational capacity, you're taking responsibility for the capacity of your entire team. The example of my brother and the hostile parents demonstrates this point. As he participated in the parent-teacher conference in a balanced, healthy, mindful way, everyone else at the table was influenced by his approach. So master your mind and your mouth by tempering your minimizing tendency with greater candor and courage, and your win tendency with greater curiosity and humility. Be a productive variable in your team.

Teamwork

By treating dialogue as a discipline, a team can breathe new life into every aspect of its work—from running meetings, making decisions, managing people, and solving problems to implementing strategy and orchestrating change. Developing this mindful approach is not an activity separate from working, managing, and leading; it's an integral part of it. A team best acquires these skills as it applies them to its regular activities. To that end, what follows is a set of proven strategies for helping teams build this discipline and bake it into their work culture.

Meeting time is practice time. Every meeting should have a dual focus on both making informed decisions and on making them in an increasingly effective manner. One executive framed it to his team this way: "I want our ability to work in the sweet spot to improve with every meeting, so from here on the primary purpose of our meetings is to practice these skills. Of course, to do that we'll have to solve problems, make decisions, deal with conflicts, and the like. But I want our focus on how we do those things, not just on doing them."

Decision making. Every decision provides an opportunity for practice. Remember, balanced dialogue is not about talking until everyone on the team reaches agreement; it's about helping the person making the decision make the most informed and effective choice possible. So if you find yourself in a meeting and you're not sure what the decision is, or who is responsible for making it, that should be your first inquiry.

Here are some tips for effective dialogue and decision making:

1. Clearly state the decision that needs to be made and who is responsible for making it.

2. Only involve people who need to be involved.

3. Share the decision-maker's current position and thinking, even if that position is fuzzy. For example, a manager might say, "I need to make a decision about X. To start the conversation, let me share the reason I'm currently torn between two options, and then I'd like some rigorous input from the team to help me clarify my thinking."

4. Put a time limit on the discussions. Spend enough time to get different views in the open, but don't waste time trying to reach agreement. Once you have enough information on the table to help the decision maker make an informed choice, move on to the next issue. If you realize you need more information or analysis, ask people to do their homework and schedule a time to revisit the decision.

Prepare for implementation. When a decision is made, explore what conversations might need to occur to ensure it's well implemented. Who will the decision impact, and what conversations will you need to have with them? Ask people responsible for those conversations if they need any practice or coaching to help them prepare. In this way, you're not just using the skills to make decisions but to ensure they're implemented effectively.

Use visual reminders. Many teams use posters or other visual cues to help remind people of the skills and their importance to balanced teamwork. One client has the ladder of inference on the wall in every meeting room in the building, a reminder of how easily people can see the same situation so differently. This helps reinforce team members' need to actively inquire into views that differ from their own. It's not uncommon to hear someone inquire in their meetings by saying, "Can you please bring your point down the ladder?" Still other teams have the sweet spot, and the four skills for candor and curiosity, plainly illustrated. It doesn't have to be so formal. You can just as easily jot the four skills on a flip chart before addressing a tough issue in a meeting. No matter how you do it, using visuals helps us overcome our old tendencies and learn new ones, much in the way "look right," and "look left" painted on curbs help people manage their habitual tendency to look the wrong way when stepping into the street in a foreign country.

Jointly design how to use the skills in your team. A team leader with a superb grasp of the candor skills promised to do more testing on inquiry to balance out his brusque style. "But I guarantee you I'll forget in the heat of the moment, " he said. "We need to figure out a way you can all remind me." His team members agreed on a "time-out" hand signal to help their boss realize when it was necessary to balance his push with more pull. In this way the entire team was helping him manage his tendency. Still another person asked a close colleague to help him in meetings: "If I forgot to test and inquire, please jump in and test or inquire for me." A person struggling with their minimize tendency might say, "If you suspect I'm holding onto a view, inquire into it and help me get it into the meeting." A question you and your team might explore is this: "What do we need more and less of in our meetings and conversations so we're getting better and better at using these skills?"

Help each other. In a jazz performance, a big part of being a top performer is the ability to accompany, or "comp," the other musicians, to both support and provoke them to play at their best.[10] When it comes to disciplined dialogue, you do this by listening to what's being played, and then playing what's missing. If your colleague puts forward a view but fails to explain or test it, you can inquire to help him maintain balance: "John, you've said you think the decision is a bad one, and I'd be curious to hear more about why you think that. Can you give us an example or two?" In this way, team members can support a colleague who's not handling himself in a balanced manner by compensating for his lapse of skill. If someone puts forward a position but fails to explain it, you inquire. If a colleague puts forward her position and thinking but fails to test, you jump in and test for her. It boosts a team's collective confidence when everyone knows teammates will jump in to "comp" whenever one team member loses discipline.

Appoint a monitor or facilitator. Some groups appoint a conversational capacity "monitor" in meetings, a role that rotates between all members of the team. The monitor's job is to track how well the team is using the skills and to provide periodic feedback. Still other teams prefer a more hands-on approach, so at the beginning of each meeting they appoint a facilitator who's authorized to make interventions to help hold the team in the sweet spot.

Create a code of conversational conduct. Many teams jointly design a formal agreement for how they'll operate, how they'll hold each other accountable, and how they'll catch themselves and self-correct whenever they slide back into old habits. A private school in New England agreed on a set of operating principles by which they'd work together. The list included the following:

> ➤ No untested attributions. It's okay to make assumptions, just test them.

> ➤ No personal attacks or dismissive behaviors (tone, body language, or words).

> ➤ Have a bias toward conversation, not e-mail. Only use e-mail for the dissemination of information, not for solving problems or airing disagreements.

> ➤ Keep open dialogue and informed choice as your highest goal, not ego-satisfaction or being "right" or safe.

➤ Make respect, compassion, curiosity, and a quest for the higher good key drivers of your behavioral choices.

➤ Balance your push and pull. Bring more attention and discipline to how you participate in discussions. No steamrolling, dominating, or withholding.

➤ If someone fails to test, jump in and test for them. Don't chastise them for not testing or roll your eyes and adopt a critical demeanor.

➤ If you have an issue with X, go talk to X. No backbiting or "hallway" dynamics.

➤ If you're not able to reach a solution or make progress, ask a third party for help.

➤ Address breeches of this protocol immediately. Hold each other accountable for these agreements. If you don't point out when someone has violated an agreement, you're enabling the behavior.

Hold each other accountable. Position. Thinking. Testing. Inquiry. You can tell when team members are using these skills and when they're not. It's observable, measurable behavior, so team members can hold each other accountable for using these skills in meetings. Track it. Monitor it. Provide each other feedback, and use it as another opportunity for practice. If a team member is not doing any testing in meetings, a concerned colleague might have a private conversation with him and raise it as an issue—especially if the lack of testing violates a team agreement. When someone is doing a good job using the skills, point that out, too.

Practice regularly. Find issues or predicaments on which you can focus for practice. An architectural firm practiced the skills by getting people to explore ways to push back on clients in a productive way. The firm had a strong minimizing culture and leaders found they were often making costly changes on projects without seeking compensation because they were too "nice." They wanted to learn how to push back using the skills, to engage in a dialogue with their clients when a change was requested. To do this, they pulled their key people to an offsite meeting where they scripted out a few basic approaches and then practiced by role-playing in triads. In one day, the team developed a plethora of ways to respond productively when a client requested a change, and because of the practice, the skill level of the entire group increased significantly.

Acknowledge and reward people. Acknowledge and reward people who are making a genuine effort, and do it both publicly and privately. "I tested a view earlier, and Jane took me up on it and pushed back. I know that wasn't easy, and I'm grateful you did it. I'm hoping to see more of that kind of behavior from everyone around the table as time goes on." A couple of my clients use the last few minutes of every meeting to provide feedback to those people who are using the skills well. "John, when I tested my perspective on point X, I didn't do a very good job, and yet you still took me up on it. I know that wasn't easy, and I wanted you to know I appreciate it." When people recognize the behaviors are valued and rewarded, they'll invest more time in learning to acquire and use them.

An Upward Spiral of Performance

The more we practice, the better we get at recognizing our mindless, habituated, automatic reactions and taming them with an intentional set of skilled behaviors. The goal is to kick start an "adoptive loop" in which using the skills leads to higher learning and effectiveness, which in turn reinforces the mindset, making it even more likely we'll continue using the skills.

The Power of One

All team members do not have to be equally skilled for the conversational capacity of a team to increase, nor is it dependent on everyone having the same level of commitment to using the skills. It's not even necessary that everyone on the team be aware of the skills. One or two people can have a dramatic impact on a team's performance by simply carrying more of the burden for keeping the team in the sweet spot. How do they do that? The same way Airto Moreira plays jazz, by listening to what's being played in a conversation and then playing what's missing. When someone puts out a naked position, they inquire into it. When someone forgets to test, they jump in and test for that person. When they put forward their own perspective they shore up the conversational capacity of the team by intentionally balancing their push and their pull.

Don't Hold Off

Remember, we shouldn't wait for a crisis before we start building our capacity and that of our team. We can use little issues that arise each day—minor conflicts, differences of opinion, lesser problems and decisions—as opportunities for practice so that when a more pressing issue inevitably hits the table, we're more equipped to handle it.

Remain Positive

We should remain positive even when we slip up. A close friend and colleague, Frank Barrett, wrote a book that describes a key heuristic of brilliant jazz performers: They adopt an attitude of saying *"Yes to the Mess."*[11] In jazz, a mistake is seen as an opportunity, not a disaster, a chance to take the performance in new, unexpected directions, to jointly create something fresh, original, and unscripted. In jazz, as Miles Davis put it, "If you're not making a mistake, it's a mistake."[12]

So it is with learning these skills. If we're not making a mistake, it's a mistake. When we fall back into our old habits, we should say yes to the mess, see what we can learn, and move on. We shouldn't beat ourselves up over our minimize and win tendencies. Recognize that they're a part of us, that they often conflict with other intentions, and that we have to keep an eye on them. It's also important to adopt a constructive, learning-oriented mindset by taking note of our strengths and not just bemoaning our weaknesses. A conversation I had with an executive in Seattle provides a case in point. "My win tendency is too strong," he told me in a workshop.

"Don't be overly hard on yourself," I suggested. "Try reframing it this way: you're exceptionally good with the candor skills. Your goal now is to put in enough practice so you're just as proficient with the curiosity skills."

It's Worth It

A competency that requires this much effort to acquire doesn't appeal to everyone. Many people prefer to avoid the hard look in the mirror that this discipline demands. They shy away from the work required to switch off their behavioral autopilot—the very thing they need to do to become more mindful and purposeful in their interactions with others. But for those of us who stick with the practice and build our discipline, the rewards we reap, both personally and professionally, pay off in multiple ways. We don't leave our conversational capacity on our desks when we leave the workplace at night; we take it with us to every situation, role, issue, and conversation we encounter in life.

9

Conversational Capacity and the Challenge of Team Leadership

An organization is a community of discourse.
Leadership is about shaping the nature
of the discourse.

ROBERT KEGAN

This book is about building teams that perform when the pressure is on, and the vital role conversational capacity plays in building such teams. In an exploration of this subject we can't ignore the issue of team leadership, a function that is often defined in simple terms—as a role performed by a person in charge. But in this chapter we'll consider a double-loop way of framing what constitutes real team leadership—as an activity far more complex and challenging than just being assigned a slot in the hierarchy. Specifically, we'll explore four key distinctions. Effective team leadership:

➤ Focuses the team on the appropriate challenge

➤ Ensures that the team has sufficient conversational capacity to engage the challenge

> ➤ Is not the same as authority
> ➤ Rarely comes from just one person

Focusing the Team on the Appropriate Challenge

Even if the conversational capacity of our team is high, we won't get far if we're concentrating on the wrong problem. An essential task of effective team leadership, therefore, is to focus the team on the *appropriate challenge*. We'll waste loads of time, energy, and money if we're changing our organization's structure when the real problem is our organization's culture.

This may sound obvious, but it's harder than you might expect. To understand why, let's again look at the two fundamental kinds of problems I put forward in the Introduction. One is a *routine problem*,[1] which can be difficult and bothersome, but for which we have ready experts and proven solutions on which we can depend for a fix. In other words, a routine problem is routine not because it happens regularly but because we have a routine for dealing with it. Routine problems can be frustrating and expensive, but they're routine in that we have an established remedy at hand. If our computer crashes or our car breaks down, there's an expert we can call to help us diagnose and fix the problem.

Far from routine, an *adaptive challenge* is a problem for which there are no easy answers,[2] no proven routines for dealing with the issue, no expert who can ride in and save the day. If a broken computer is a routine problem, a soured corporate culture is an adaptive one. An executive team can't just mandate a fresh culture. There is no cultural Jiffy Lube staffed with experts who can flush out our old culture and replace it with a new one. For a culture to change, people all around the company have to roll up their sleeves and find healthier ways of communicating and working together. This is far more demanding work.

An organization in a stable state, with little change or challenge, may face a preponderance of routine issues. But an organization dealing with growth, change, competition, limited resources, and other unwelcome realities[3] often faces a number of adaptive hurdles. This might include (but is certainly not limited to) poor working relationships between people and groups; a corporate culture that stifles the strategy; a colleague who is technically brilliant but socially corrosive; or a competency gap where the skills that served us well in the past are not the skills that will propel us into the future.

Adaptive Work

The distinction between routine and adaptive predicaments is important because the work required to address them is fundamentally different. We have to carefully sort our way through an adaptive challenge because we're in uncharted territory, where our old ways of thinking and operating won't help us solve the problem. "The work the people must do to progress in the face of an adaptive challenge is simply called *adaptive work*,"[4] says Dean Williams. While there's a prevailing policy, expert, or procedure we can utilize in a routine predicament, facilitating adaptive work is a more arduous undertaking. The absence of a clear path forward requires we work with others to make sense of the unfamiliar problem we're facing— a messy process that involves grappling with what Jim Collins and his research team refer to as "the brutal facts" of our current reality[5] —and then working hard to orchestrate the hard changes required to adapt to those brutal facts.

"The resolution of an adaptive challenge," says Dean Williams, "requires a shift in values and mindsets,"[6] so high conversational capacity, and the double-loop learning it enables, is indispensable for doing adaptive work. To get our bearings in an unfamiliar predicament, we need to get the "cops" and the "architects" working together to generate a more useful map of the adaptive terrain we must traverse. Ron Heifetz explains it this way: "Someone exercising leadership is orchestrating the process of getting factions with competing definitions of the problem to start learning from one another."[7]

Partly because we lack the distinction, and partly because this work is so challenging, we often treat an adaptive challenge as if it's a routine problem. After the *Challenger* disaster in 1988, for example, NASA focused on changing rules, structure, protocols, and procedures but failed to address the organization's culture and its impact on communication and decision making. They ignored the deeper issue described by Chris Argyris. "The problems were not only in the structure, rules, and independent monitoring devices. The problems also were that highly committed, well-intentioned, safety-oriented, can-do players reasoned and acted in ways that violated their own standards and made certain that this violation was covered up and that the cover-up was covered up."[8] Richard Feynman, the renowned physicist and Nobel laureate who was a member of the committee that investigated the *Challenger* disaster, put it this way: "Well, it's one thing to figure out what went wrong with the shuttle. But the next thing would be to find out what was the matter with the organization of NASA."[9] Argyris and Feynman both recognized that fine-tuning safety procedures is relatively technical and routine, while addressing the organization's counterproductive culture is more difficult and adaptive.

Checklists

Dr. Atul Gawande, a surgeon and the author of *The Checklist Manifesto*, describes the challenge posed by getting doctors and their teams to use surgical checklists. Research shows that asking simple questions before each surgery, "such as 'Did we give the patient her antibiotic?' and, 'Did we introduce ourselves to one another?' can reduce infections and deaths by more than a third."[10]

But while at first glance implementing the use of simple checklists may seem routine, getting doctors to actually use them requires an adaptive shift in the culture of healthcare. The use of checklists is often "met with hostility, because it challenges doctors' cherished notions about status, autonomy, and expertise," says Gawande. "Many surgeons feel asking such questions to be 'beneath them.'" The culture in hospitals and healthcare reinforces the notion of doctors as individuals, rather than as an integrated part of a healthcare team. "We're celebrated cowboys, but what we need is more pit crews," says Gawande. Creating a checklist is routine, but getting doctors to embrace their use requires an adaptive change in the *culture* of healthcare and a double-loop shift in how doctors frame their roles in the system.

We saw this same propensity to treat an adaptive challenge as if it's routine in Chapter 1 when the executive team ran into trouble implementing its new strategy. The executives were all smart people; they all agreed their new strategy was the key to greater growth and profitability; and they were all experienced, technically savvy managers. Yet implementation floundered because people, including the very executives who were most committed to the strategy, resisted the kinds of sacrifices needed to carry it out. They treated the implementation process like a routine checklist, and failed to address its more adaptive aspects—their corporate culture, their old habits, and their instinctively defensive reactions to change.

We Avoid Adaptive Work

Because adaptive work forces us to face harsh realities and make difficult changes, we tend to avoid it like the crazy aunt at a family reunion. So it takes courage to get people to surface and engage unpleasant, stressful, and unfamiliar realities. "The real heroism of leadership involves having the courage to face reality—and helping the people around you to face reality," says Heifetz. "Mustering the courage to interrogate reality is a central function of a leader. And that requires the courage to face three realities at once. First, what values do we stand for—and are there gaps between those values and how we actually behave? Second, what are the skills and talents of our company—and are there gaps between those resources and what the market demands? Third, what opportunities does the future hold—and are there gaps between those opportunities and our ability to capitalize on them?"[11]

Seeking answers to such questions is rarely a stress-free undertaking, and doing it well requires a heightened capacity for balancing candor with curiosity, and courage with humility. When our team's conversational capacity is anemic, it's tempting to redefine the problem as routine, as an issue our team can actually handle. Rather than increase our capacity to meet the challenge, we redefine the problem to fit our capacity. The kind of problems we're able to solve, in other words, is constrained by our ability to productively discuss them.

Ego

Our ego is another reason we avoid adaptive work. Not wanting to look like we can't handle the problem, or to come across as clueless, apathetic, or afraid, we *pretend* we know what to do and opt for a quick fix, creating the temporary illusion of progress, as if we're doing something about the problem and making headway. But this is the opposite of real team leadership because we're helping people sidestep the adaptive work they need to undertake.

Further exacerbating this tendency to frame an adaptive predicament as routine is the fear that we'll be "Galileo-ed" if we call too much attention to the unwelcome realities we're facing. We minimize the scale of the problem, pretending to have an answer, afraid that if we don't, the powers that be will just find someone who will.

The Problem Is Erroneously Defined

And if all this wasn't enough, we often avoid adaptive work simply because we've erroneously assumed the problem we're up against is routine. This was the problem with the CEO who first framed his leadership issue as a routine problem and spent lots of time and money on a search for the right HR person to help him fix it. He looked at the problem as something outside of himself that didn't require any shifts in his attitudes, beliefs, or behaviors. "Simply find the right person with the right strategy," he assumed, "and my problem is solved." He recognized the adaptive nature of his predicament when he accepted the unwelcome reality that his own behavior, and that of his executive team, was the primary obstacle to the business performance he was seeking. It was only when he focused on the appropriate challenge that meaningful progress was possible.

Ensuring That the Team Has the Conversational Capacity to Engage the Challenge

Harry Truman, speaking about his relationship with congress, aptly articulated a major reason adaptive work is so challenging; "I don't give 'em hell," he once said about congress, "I just tell the truth, and they think it's hell." That's an excellent summary of the basic problem: facing harsh realities and difficult changes often hurts like hell. And if the tensions and conflicts provoked by adaptive work are greater than our team's capacity for dealing with them, we're in trouble before we even start. So building the conversational capacity of our team is an essential aspect of adaptive leadership. It makes no sense to march our team into a challenging predicament it's ill equipped to handle.

The reason conversational capacity is so vital in an adaptive context is that in order to double-loop learn we must lean into conflicting perspectives that tend to trigger our defensive reactions. "Leaders of the future need to have the stomach for conflict and uncertainty—among their people and within themselves," says Heifetz. But, he points out, "Companies tend to be allergic to conflict—particularly companies that have been in operation for a long time. Being averse to conflict is understandable. Conflict is dangerous: It can damage relationships. It can threaten friendships. But conflict is the primary engine of creativity and innovation. People don't learn by staring into a mirror; people learn by encountering difference. So hand in hand with the courage to face reality comes the courage to surface and orchestrate conflicts."[12] To exercise leadership, we need to get people with contrasting ladders of inference to communicate in a way that expands how we're thinking about the challenge we're facing. This, in turn, requires high conversational capacity because without it, the conflict is wasted. It elicits no double-loop learning.

Don't Kill the Goose

A small company in California faced an adaptive challenge that threatened the very life of the firm. The company's socially conscious, laid-back culture attracted intelligent, motivated people who ensured the company flourished. Their success led to substantial growth, and soon it became obvious their old ways of doing things just wouldn't scale. With this in mind, the CEO unilaterally introduced more process and procedure to better manage the expanding enterprise. But the increased structure and process threatened the very culture that had made the firm successful in the first place, and the highly committed people who had been attracted to the business now complained that it was changing. "If I wanted to work for IBM, I would have applied there," snapped one frustrated manager. There was no simple solution for the adaptive challenge they faced: how to grow and expand the company *without* killing the goose that lays the golden egg—their unique culture.

To deal with this challenge, the CEO shifted her approach by doing two things. First, she systematically bolstered the conversational capacity of her managers by putting them through a series of workshops designed to help them practice the skills as they addressed real issues. Second, she then focused her people on the primary dilemma: how to make necessary changes without destroying the culture. She did this in a way that should seem familiar: She put forward her ideas for change, laid out the reasoning behind them, and then asked for the input and suggestions of her people. Rather than sit back and complain about the changes she was making, her people now had to pull together and come up with better ones.

It worked. Because she'd invested in their capacity to work in the sweet spot, her people pulled together, double-loop learned, and successfully managed the precarious adjustment from entrepreneurial start-up to a more mature enterprise. More impressively, they did so in a way that actually strengthened their distinct culture. The goose survived, and their success continues to this day.

Be Proactive

It's best to build the capacity of a team before an adaptive challenge hits the fan. An engineering company that tried to increase the team abilities to work in the sweet spot *after* they'd reached a dreadful level of dysfunction found it was almost impossible to recover. The firm's belated attempt to build their conversational capacity was swamped by the tensions, frictions, low trust, and soured relationships infecting the teams. With skepticism, frustration, and cynicism high, they were stuck in a horrible climate for learning and applying the skills. They faced a catch-22: They needed the skills to climb out of their dysfunction, but they were too overwhelmed by their dysfunction to acquire the skills. In workshops, we'd put them in breakout groups to practice as they grappled with real issues, but they'd ignore the "practice" and merely argue about the issues. They eventually made headway, but they spent more time and money for less progress and skill than if they'd invested in their conversational capacity *before* they'd gone off the rails.

Contrast that experience with the executive team at a thriving marketing company that worked hard to foster a corporate culture characterized by high conversational capacity and double-loop learning *before* it faced any adaptive crises. Successful and growing, these bright team members recognized that this was no time to coast, and they invested in their capacity for working together more effectively under stress. Members of the executive team started first, learning the skills and then using their day-to-day interactions to increase their competence. The rest of management came next, and soon the entire company was trained in the skills. Framed posters popped up around the business with key concepts like the sweet spot, the ladder of inference, the four basic skills, and double-loop learning, and they used the skills to run more effective meetings, make better decisions, solve tough problems, and design healthier work relationships between different people and functions throughout the enterprise. They also started using this discipline to foster more vibrant and flexible relationships with their clients.

After two years of work and practice, they were more prepared when their big adaptive challenge hit. When they made the strategic decision to sever the relationship with their largest customer—who was increasingly abusive, arrogant, and tightfisted (and consequently less and less profitable)—the entire company pulled together, viewing the difficult change as an opportunity rather than a crisis. "This is a customer we want our competition to have," one executive told me. Despite the pressure they were under, the company was able to squarely face the brutal facts of their new reality and make painful adjustments to realign their business with the new challenges they were facing. They reacted constructively to their adaptive predicament because they had proactively geared up to deal with it.

Leadership Is Not the Same as Authority

Leadership is *not* the same as authority. This can be a hard concept to grasp because we usually lump the two together. "John is our CEO," an employee might say, "so he's our leader." In his role as CEO there is no doubt John has formal authority, but whether or not he uses his authority to exercise leadership is a very different question. Kenneth Lay and Jeffrey Skilling, the top executives at Enron, had lots of authority, but few people would argue that they exercised any leadership. Others, like Mahatma Gandhi and Martin Luther King, Jr., enjoyed no formal authority, but few would argue that they didn't exercise profound leadership.

So if it's different from authority, what does it mean to exercise leadership? Is it just a matter of getting people to do what we want? Is leadership merely a synonym for influence? Is it simply the process of creating a vision and convincing people to follow it? Is the Pied Piper, in other words, an appropriate metaphor for leadership? If we accept that definition, then we have to admit that the first lemming off the cliff is exercising leadership. No, there's a better way to frame it.

Real Team Leadership Is About Orchestrating Learning

Adaptive leadership[13] is not about coming up with an idea or solution and then convincing the group to adopt it. It's about orchestrating a process of learning that gets people with different views and agendas learning from each other as they tackle an adaptive challenge.

But when we're faced with an adaptive challenge, we often want just the opposite. We yearn for someone to scream out, "Don't worry. I know what to do," someone who says he or she has a plan for resolving our messy predicament. "In a crisis we tend to look for the wrong kind of leadership," says Heifetz. "We call for someone with answers, decision, strength, and a map of the future, someone who knows where we ought to be going—in short, someone who can make hard problems simple."[14] But this is wishful thinking. No such person exists, and anyone saying differently is selling (or slinging) something.

We All Can Lead

When we equate leadership with authority, we disempower a huge swath of people who can help orchestrate adaptive change. But when we liberate leadership from authority we empower *anyone* who wants to foment productive change because we realize that while authority is *assigned* to us by the organization, leadership is an activity we *choose*. Seen this way, leadership can be exercised from any point in the system. It's not the sole responsibility of the authorities. I like how Heifetz puts it: "A president and a clerk can both lead."[15]

Remember the CEO who double-loop learned and declared, "I now realize that the very people I'm trying to attract to my business *will not work for someone like me*." Armed with this significant "aha," he dug into the adaptive work of changing his team's operating assumptions and behavior in order to cultivate a healthier business culture. He did this from his *position of authority*.

The Flamethrower, on the other hand, had no formal authority with his colleagues. But as a lay member of his team, he exercised leadership by working hard to shift his own behavior and the dynamics in his work group. In both examples we see the same activity—fostering double-loop learning and adaptive work—but from different positions within their respective organizations.

No matter who we are, or where we stand in the pecking order, if we're building the conversational capacity of our team and focusing that capacity on an adaptive challenge, we're exercising team leadership. Leadership is not about the roles we're formally assigned; it's about the roles we choose to perform.

Effective Team Leadership Rarely Comes from Just One Person

The fourth and final distinction is this: Leadership rarely comes from just one person. Despite the popular myth of the solo leader, several people often "team up" to provide the leadership needed. Real *team* leadership, in other words, comes from a team. When he took on the adaptive challenges facing India, Mahatma Gandhi didn't act alone—he worked with a trusted team of people, including many who had different views about how to approach those challenges. Similarly, Abraham Lincoln used his "team of rivals," and their conflicting political perspectives, to help him navigate the extraordinarily adaptive terrain facing the United States during the Civil War.

When the Flamethrower changed the way he interacted with his team he didn't do it by himself. A couple of his teammates, eager to see things improve, assisted him with the task. They reminded him to test when he forgot, and they inquired into his views when he failed to share his thinking. When the Flamethrower tested a view, his partners exercised courage by pushing back on it. They sought no credit for their efforts, but their assistance was instrumental in helping build a healthier team dynamic.

This way of framing team leadership conflicts with the popular view that leadership comes from a person riding in on a white horse to save the day. But it's this cowboy notion of leadership that Dr. Gawande says needs to change if using checklists is to become a regular part of the culture in surgical teams: "Think of Sully Sullenberger, the pilot who landed that plane on the Hudson River. The way the public saw him was similar to how it wants to see doctors and how doctors want to see themselves. The story the public had about him was that he was an unbelievable pilot, and that's what saved the plane. He was the hero. But he kept saying no, it was adherence to protocol and teamwork that allowed us to safely land the plane. In a similar way, heroism in medicine means having the humility to recognize that we are more likely to fail on our own, and *embracing teamwork to help us provide the best care.*"[16] Leadership in surgery, in other words, doesn't come from the brilliant surgeon alone, but from the team of people working together on behalf of the patient. The key is to orchestrate a process that gets everyone on the same page (literally, in the case of checklists) and working together on behalf of the patient.

It's the same in all our teams and organizations. We often expect our team leaders, managers, and executives to step in and save the day with the right answer. And when we're in a position of authority, we often—consciously or not—expect ourselves to play that cowboy role. But while finding and following a person with "the answers" may work when we're facing simple, routine problems, it's a disaster when the challenge is more complex and adaptive. In fact, if the problem is so simple that a person with a clear answer can drop in and solve the problem, it's routine by definition, and no leadership is required to solve it. When the challenge can only be met when a group of people "team up" to make adaptive

changes to their culture or community, leadership is always necessary to solve the problem.

Consider the chair of the board of a private school facing a
community rife with conflict between the faculty, administration,
and parents. She dealt with the problem by first encouraging each
of these groups to invest significant time and resources to bolster
their conversational capacity, and then by encouraging them to focus that capacity on improving the working relationships *within*
and *between* the three groups. The double-loop learning she orchestrated produced growing levels of cooperation and commitment between the previously warring factions and transformed the
school community.

She didn't do this alone. She partnered with other board members, consultants, members of the administration, key members of
the faculty, and concerned parents by pulling them into the process,
seeking their input and counsel, and involving them in designing
interventions to turn the school around. She was often quietly orchestrating this process in the background, purposefully avoiding
too much involvement in the various activities, precisely because
she didn't want this to be seen as an effort that belonged to the
board chair. She knew that for the process to succeed the work
had to come largely from the community itself. It took time and
persistence, but the work she and her colleagues orchestrated paid
off. The school community gradually transformed as they rebuilt
damaged relationships, established new protocols for acceptable behavior in the community (including the skills for working in the
sweet spot), and refocused everyone on their shared goal—building
a thriving school community where children flourish and grow.

Faulty Claims

Team leadership works the same way in any business. A large insurance company asked an outside firm to conduct rigorous bench-

marking assessments to gather information about performance in key areas of the business. One area that was thoroughly assessed was the claims department, and the picture of performance that developed was not flattering. While claims officers described themselves as "without a doubt the best in the field," the statistics showed quite convincingly that they were handling claims more slowly, and making higher settlements, than about 85 percent of the industry.

The senior manager of the claims department, Peter, refused to share this unwelcome information with the claims staff, assuming that because the assessment radically contradicted their perceptions, the feedback would crush staff morale. Unilaterally acting on his assumption, Peter initiated a change process to deal with the secret problem. Not surprisingly, the staff, who felt things were just fine, strongly resisted what they perceived as unnecessary changes. "Why fix something if it's not broken?" they complained. When it became clear that Peter would not back down, the staff started chewing "corn nuts," bad-mouthing management, filing complaints with HR, and vigorously resisting the changes.

The escalating battle created a hostile environment where staff mistrusted management and management mistrusted staff, making it even less likely that Peter would divulge the secret data because in such a hostile environment he believed it would be received very cynically. Peter's unilateral attempts to improve the business were being defeated by the staff, and the atmosphere had been poisoned, making any future changes even more difficult to implement. The business was in serious trouble.

To make matters worse, the line managers who reported to Peter held strongly different views as to whether or not the staff should be apprised of the situation. This disagreement was rarely discussed openly and created strong, subterranean divisions in the management team itself. Instead of raising concerns in the team where debate could be had, line managers complained to staff, other managers outside the department, and even some customers. Managers heard through the grapevine that some of their peers held differing views, but the fact that they were aware of these differences was also covered up and avoided. As a result the tensions began to fester.

Peter heard of various rumors and grumblings and raised them with his team. But the line managers minimized by covering up their concerns and feigning support for the change process.

It was at this point that top executives, alarmed by the growing dysfunction in the claims department, brought in organizational development professionals to help the entire claims department. Impressively, rather than get defensive and resist the assistance, the managers pulled together, worked incredibly hard to build their conversational capacity. They then set to work engaging the tough issues they had to confront by teaming up to do the adaptive work.

One outspoken line manager, Mike, asked the tough questions and called attention to the unwelcome realities that had been hitherto avoided. His forceful, direct personality made him the perfect point person for this task. Peter, as the senior manager, regulated Mike's interventions to keep the conversations from overheating. He called for breaks when things became overly tense or put a hold on discussions so more data could be gathered: "We're out of time. Let's gather more information on this and give people time to reflect. I suggest we get back together on Wednesday to explore this decision in more detail."

One of Mike's fellow managers, Tina, lent indispensable support by helping him test his views when he failed to remember, and by making sure he was not the only one in the team bringing up the hot subjects (which could have gotten him labeled a troublemaker or malcontent, thus limiting his effectiveness). Tina also spent untold hours behind the scenes listening to concerns, smoothing ruffled feathers, and keeping people engaged in the learning.

This trio worked together to do the requisite adaptive work—rebuilding relationships, earning back trust, improving how they interacted with each other, and resolving festering conflicts. They also helped each other push the change into their respective departments—cofacilitating workshops to help their people learn the skills as they tackled real issues—thereby building the conversational capacity of the entire claims unit. The process unfolded over many months, but the changes they orchestrated were so significant that they eventually won a top quality award, the first of its kind in their industry. Mike, a young line manager at the time, eventually went on to become CEO of the company.

Building Conversational Capacity Is an Adaptive Challenge

Team leadership is a demanding task. It requires getting people to face tough realities they'd rather avoid, and to make the tough changes required to adapt to those realities. Motivating people to change their behavior is challenge enough, but adaptive work requires deeper shifts in their values, beliefs, assumptions, and norms. It requires, in other words, double-loop learning. Orchestrating such change is difficult because while people want adaptive challenges solved, they almost always want them solved by someone else, or at least to have the experience be pain free. "With or without authority, exercising leadership is risky and difficult," says Heifetz. "Instead of providing answers as a means of direction, sometimes the best you can do is provide questions, or face people with the hard facts, instead of protecting people from change."[17]

Here again we face the same dilemma. Staring unwelcome realities straight in the face can easily trigger strong defensive reactions. Rather than focus on the issues, people will often focus on each other, blaming colleagues, functions, and management for the situations they're in. This is exactly what happened with the executives in Chapter 1, who all agreed on the hard changes needed to implement their shiny new strategy, but only as long as it was *everyone else* who did the changing. They all wanted to head in the same strategic direction, but they balked when confronted with the unpleasant reality that they'd have to make substantial changes to how they ran and led their own part of the business. Lacking sufficient conversational capacity, their defensive reactions overwhelmed their abilities to implement the strategy.

Doing adaptive work requires the ability to curb our well-honed defensive tendencies and remain balanced under pressure. But this presents us with a paradox, for the task of building this discipline is itself an adaptive challenge. Conversational capacity isn't like milk or eggs; we can't just buy a fresh carton when we're running low. Building it requires far more than just adopting a behavioral checklist—it requires that we rein in our powerful minimizing and winning tendencies and let our commitment to informed choice guide our behavior. It doesn't get more adaptive than that.

Our Better Angels

Framed this way, team leadership provides another way to exercise our better angels. The desire to play the role of the larger-than-life, "I've got all the answers" solo leader receives much of his energy from hubris and conceit. But when we admit that we need to work closely with others to address an adaptive issue—the essence of true team leadership—our approach is driven more by curiosity and humility. We're more problem-centric and less egocentric, more open-minded and less, "I've got it all figured out." More Lincoln and less Pied Piper.

The same is also true of our *response* to someone who claims to have all the answers. The whole sad routine in which a domineering egotist declares, "I have the answers to all your problems" and a group of fainthearted followers fall in line behind him is just another manifestation of the min-win dynamic we've been exploring. A person with an inflated ego and a strong opinion says, "I know exactly what to do," and a flock of people passively minimize by going along with the unadulterated bullshit he's slinging—even when they know, deep down inside, it's not going to work.[18] When we succumb to our tendencies toward conformity and timidity and submit to a pseudo-leader, we abdicate our responsibility for focusing the group on the adaptive challenge it's facing. We become an accomplice in helping the group avoid the real work required to move forward.

But when we use the discipline to help orchestrate a learning process that pulls our team together around the adaptive challenges it's facing, we're taking responsibility for the hard work our team needs to tackle, and, in the process, we're exercising our better angels.

What Are Your Challenges?

To tie the learning to your unique circumstances and challenges, here are some questions for you and your team to consider:

➤ What are the adaptive challenges facing you and your team?

➤ What are the unwelcome realities associated with those challenges?

➤ Is your team's conversational capacity sufficient for doing the requisite adaptive work? Where is "the line" in your team's list of tough issues, decisions, conflicts, and challenges?

➤ What can you bring to key conversations to help build the conversational capacity of your team? What is being played, and how can you play what's missing?

➤ What work will you have to do to ensure you have the capacity to communicate in a balanced, disciplined way when the pressure is on?

➤ Do you have partners who can help you orchestrate the adaptive work?

➤ How can you jointly design how you and your partners will "team up" to facilitate that work?

These are important questions to consider. We can no longer afford our antiquated, one-dimensional, cartoonish notions of leadership because our world is growing more interconnected, dynamic, and unpredictable, and the number of adaptive challenges we face continues to escalate. There is, therefore, a growing need for highly effective teams who have the capacity to address tough, messy, unfamiliar problems with great skill and confidence. It is my sincere hope you'll use the ideas in this book to help build one.

Conclusion:
The Road Less
Traveled

....

We're our own dragons as well as our own heroes,
and we have to rescue ourselves from ourselves.

TOM ROBBINS

Mythologist Joseph Campbell once said that there are only two ways to live life.[1] One is the way of the villager, a person who never strays beyond the confines of his "village," never dares to move beyond the comfort zone of his familiar, habitual patterns of living, thinking, working, and acting. The village is comfortable, predictable, and safe. We don't have to learn much to live there.

The other way to live life is the path of the hero,[2] the person who leaves her comfortable village, ventures beyond the walls of the familiar and out into the great unknown in pursuit of more expansive ways of living, working, thinking, and acting.

Myths teach us that whenever we set forth from a village—be it mental, vocational, behavioral, or otherwise—we inevitably come face to face with demons hell-bent on thwarting our progress: the dragon, the Medusa, the Balrog, the flying monkeys. Campbell suggests that these menacing creatures don't represent external obstacles but our own *internal limitations*—our ignorance, incompetence, fears, hubris, and habits. If we're to move out of the village and venture successfully down the hero's path, we must conquer our demons.

Campbell's observations are instructive for the subject we've been exploring. Our habitual patterns of minimizing and winning keep us safely ensconced in our mental and behavioral village. They protect our ego and the entrenched ways of thinking and acting we use to support it. As our default set of reactions, they're easy and automatic. We don't have to learn anything to employ them. No demons block the path between us and their use.

Learning to work in the sweet spot, by contrast, is a journey set on the hero's path. Building our conversational capacity requires we vacate the ego-protective confines of our fortified village, face down our fight-or-flight demons, and side with the better angels of our nature. We must struggle to subordinate our base predilections to a higher set of values, countering our arrogance with humility, our certainty with curiosity, our caution with candor, and our timidity with courage. We remain true to our course by kicking our ego to the curb and setting our internal compass on informed choice. This is the hero's path, the road less traveled.

It's not a casual journey. Whether we're building our own capacity for working in the sweet spot, building the conversational capacity of our team, exploring conflicting ladders of inference so our team can double-loop learn, or mobilizing people to engage an adaptive challenge they'd prefer to avoid, we're a long way from the village. Whenever we choose to head down one of these daring paths we'd better have our demons in check.

The good news is that we don't have to travel this road alone. We can seek out and enroll partners, colleagues, friends, or teammates as fellow learners—people eager to head up and out of their own sheltered, self-limiting village by acquiring the mindset, learning the skills, and using both to tackle increasingly difficult issues and situations.

The journey is worth every step. Less tormented by the fight-or-flight demons that beleaguer less-disciplined souls, a *person* with these skills can elevate the performance of his or her entire team. A *team* armed with this discipline can dramatically improve its performance because team members' higher conversational capacity allows them to learn from conflict, make informed decisions, and better navigate difficult terrain. Because they're not overpowered by the defensive routines that bedevil progress in other organizations, they're better equipped to double-loop learn when they encounter wicked, complex, unprecedented challenges.

In the grand sweep of human history, our modern organizations are a recent invention, and we still have a lot to learn about building institutions that work. I wrote *Conversational Capacity* to provide a light for those people who choose to leave their village and head down the road less traveled. It maps out a way to build better, healthier, more balanced organizations, and in the process, grow to be better, healthier, more balanced *people*.

Notes

Introduction

1. Riley Sinder and Ronald Heifetz, "Political Leadership: Managing the Public's Problem Solving," in *The Power of Public Ideas*, edited by Robert Reich, Cambridge, MA: Harvard University Press, 1990, pp. 179–203. Also see Ronald Heifetz, *Leadership without Easy Answers*, Cambridge, MA: Belknap Press of Harvard University, 1994.

2. Ronald Heifetz, *Leadership without Easy Answers*, Cambridge, MA: Belknap Press of Harvard University, 1994, p. 254. See also Dean Williams, *Real Leadership*, San Francisco: Berrett-Koehler, 2005, p. 7.

Chapter 1

1. John Schwartz, "Riding Rockets: A Wide-Eyed Astronaut Becomes a NASA Critic," *New York Times*, January 24, 2006, http://www.nytimes.com/2006/01/24/science/space/24prof.html?pagewanted=print&_r=0

2. IBM. "Leading Through Connections: Insights from the Global IBM CEO Study," November 12, 2012, http://www.ibm.com/ibm/ideasfromibm/us/ceo/20080505/resources/IFI_05052008.pdf

3. Ibid.

4. Robert S. Kaplan and David P. Norton, *The Strategy-Focused Organization: How Balanced Scorecard Companies Thrive in the New Business Environment*, Cambridge, MA: Harvard Business Review Press, September 2000.

5. Lawrence Hrebiniak, *Making Strategy Work: Leading Effective Execution and Change*. Upper Saddle River, NJ: Pearson Prentice Hall, 2005.

6. Douglas LaBier, *Modern Madness*, Reading, MA: Addison-Wesley, 1986, p. 3.

7. Jeffrey Sonnenfeld, "What Makes Great Boards Great," *Harvard Business Review*, September 2002.

8. Cordelia Fine, *A Mind of Its Own: How Your Brain Distorts and Deceives*, New York: W.W. Norton, 2006, pp. 70–71.

9. Daniel Goleman, *Emotional Intelligence*, New York: Bantam, 1995, p. 148.

10. Ibid.

11. Eugene Tarnow, "Self-Destructive Obedience in the Airplane Cockpit and the Concept of Obedience Optimization," in *Obedience to Authority: Current Perspectives on the Milgram Paradigm*, edited by Blass, Mahway, NJ: Lawrence Erlbaum Associates, 2000, pp. 111–113.

12. Claudia Dreifus, "Doctor Leads Quest for Safer Ways to Care for Patients: Conversation with Dr. Peter J. Pronovost," *New York Times*, March 2010.

13. Ibid.

Chapter 2

1. Chris Argyris, *Overcoming Organizational Defenses: Facilitating Organizational Learning*, Boston: Allyn & Bacon, 1990, pp. 12–23.

2. Sarah Maslin and Nate Schweber, "A Reminder to Look(!) Both Ways," *New York Times*, September 19, 2012, http://www.nytimes.com/2012/09/20/nyregion/in-new-york-city-curbside-signs-to-look-both-ways.html?_r=0

3. Carl Sagan, *Shadows of Forgotten Ancestors*, New York: Random House, 1992, p. 110.

4. Chris Argyris and Donald A. Schön, *Theory in Practice*, San Francisco: Jossey-Bass, 1974, p. 67. Also see Chris Argyris, *Reasoning, Learning, and Action*. San Francisco: Jossey-Bass. 1982, p. 86.

5. Charles Sherrington, *The Brain and Its Mechanisms*. Rede Lecture. University Press, 1933. Quoted in Jeffrey M. Schwartz and Sharon Begley, *The Mind and the Brain*, New York: Harper-Collins, 2002, p. 54.

6. Chris Argyris and Donald A. Schön, *Organizational Learning: Theory of Action Perspective*. Reading, MA: Addison-Wesley, 1978, p. 70.

7. William Oncken, Jr. and Donald L. Wass, "Management Time: Who's Got the Monkey," *Harvard Business Review*. Reprint No. 9969 (1999). Originally published in 1974. For a deeper look at minimizing behavior and its impact, read this classic article.

8. Chris Argyris, *Overcoming Organizational Defenses: Facilitating Organizational Learning*, Boston: Allyn & Bacon, 1990, p. 13. See also Robert Putnam, Diana McLain Smith, and Chris Argyris, *Action Science*, San Francisco: Jossey-Bass, 1985, p. 83.

9. Chris Argyris, *Reasoning, Learning, and Action*, San Francisco, CA: Jossey-Bass, 1982, p. 86.

10. Chris Dade, "Baby Dies as Doctors Fight in Hospital Delivery Room," *Digital Journal*, February 26, 2010, http://m.digitaljournal .com/article/288167?doredir=0&noredir=1

11. "Baby Dies as Doctors Fight Instead of Performing Cesarean, Report Claims," *The Telegraph*, February 25, 2010, http://www .telegraph.co.uk/news/worldnews/southamerica/brazil/7318006/ Baby-dies-as-doctors-fight-instead-of-performing-Caesarean -report-claims.html

12. Steven Pinker, "The Moral Instinct," *New York Times*, January 13, 2008, http://www.nytimes.com/2008/01/13/ magazine/13Psychology-t.html?pagewanted=all

13. Edward De Bono, *Teaching Thinking*, New York: Penguin Books, 1992, pp. 72–73.

14. M. Scott Peck, *The Road Less Traveled*, New York: Simon & Schuster, 1978, pp. 67–68A; CD-ROM edition (abridged), New York: Simon & Schuster/Touchstone Books, 1998, CD2, track 02, "Balance: The Healthiness of Depression." In the CD version, read by the author, he clearly demonstrates the angry and demeaning tone he adopted in the argument.

15. Claudia Dreifus, "Doctor Leads Quest for Safer Ways to Care for Patients: A Conversation with Dr. Peter J. Pronovost," *New York Times*, March 8, 2010, http://www.nytimes.com/2010/03/09/ science/09conv.html.

16. Joan Magretta, *What Management Is*. Boston: Harvard Business School Press, 2002, p. 213.

Chapter 3

1. Chris Argyris and Donald A. Schön, *Theory in Practice*, San Francisco: John Wiley, 1974, pp. 85–89.

2. Cordelia Fine, *A Mind of Its Own*, New York: W. W. Norton, 2008, p. 108.

3. Ibid., p. 8.

4. Ibid, p. 202.

5. Scott Raab, "William Shatner: The ESQ+A," *Esquire*, February 2006, 145/2, p. 116.

6. Ron Heifetz, *Leadership without Easy Answers*, Cambridge, MA: Harvard University Press, 1994, p. 33.

7. Herman Melville, *Moby Dick: Or, the Whale*, 150th anniversary edition, New York: Penguin Books, 2001, p. 85.

8. Doris Kearns-Goodwin, *Team of Rivals*, New York: Simon & Schuster, 2005.

9. Doris Kearns-Goodwin, interview by Tim Russert, *The Tim Russert Show*, CNBC, July 2007. Television.

10. Peter Elbow, *Embracing Contraries*, New York: Oxford University Press, 1987, p. 241.

11. Chris Argyris and Donald A. Schön, *Theory in Practice*, San Francisco: John Wiley & Sons, 1974, p. 89.

12. Chris Argyris and Donald A. Schön, *Organizational Learning II*, Reading, MA: Addison-Wesley, 1996, pp. 92–95.

Chapter 4

1. Chris Argyris, *Overcoming Organizational Defenses*, Needham Heights, MA: Allyn & Bacon, 1990, pp. 104–107. See also Chris Argyris, *Reasoning, Learning, and Action,* San Francisco, CA: Jossey-Bass, 1982, pp. 102–104.

2. Airto Moreira, personal interview, April 8, 2011. Based on an initial conversation with Paul Cicco.

3. *Planes, Trains, and Automobiles*. Directed by John Hughes, with Steve Martin and John Candy, Paramount Pictures, 1987. Film.

4. Cartha DeLoach, quoted in Barbara Mikkelson, "Rumor Has It. Watch the Borders!" Snopes.com, July 9, 2007, http://www.snopes .com/language/document/borders.asp

5. M. Scott Peck, *The Road Less Traveled*, New York: Simon & Schuster, 1978, p. 32.

6. Abraham Lincoln, quoted in Alfred Fletcher Conrad, *Costs of Administering Reparation for Work Injuries in Illinois*, Urbana, IL: University of Illinois Press, 1952, p. 28.

Chapter 5

1. Daniel Kurtzman, *Stephen Colbert at the White House Correspondents' Dinner: Transcript of Colbert's Presidential Smackdown*, About.com: Political Humor, 2006, http://politicalhumor.about.com/od/

stephencolbert/a/colbertbush.htm

2. Laura Crawshaw, personal interview, 1998.

3. Abraham Lincoln, first inaugural address, March 4, 1861: "We are not enemies, but friends. We must not be enemies. Though passion may have strained it must not break our bonds of affection. The mystic chords of memory, stretching from every battlefield and patriot grave to every living heart and hearthstone all over this broad land, will yet swell the chorus of the Union, when again touched, as surely they will be, by the better angels of our nature."

4. John J. Kao, *Jamming*, New York: Harper Collins, 1997, p. 5.

5. GE 2000 Annual Report: "Informality," http://www.ge.com/annual00/, 2001, p. 7.

Chapter 6

1. This exercise is adapted from William V. Haney, *The Uncritical Inference Test*, William V. Haney Associates, 1972.

2. Chris Argyris, *Overcoming Organizational Defenses*, Needham Heights, MA: Allyn & Bacon, 1990, pp. 88–89. Also see Chris Argyris, Robert Putnam, and Diana McLain-Smith, *Action Science: Concepts, Methods, and Skills for Research and Intervention*, San Francisco: Jossey-Bass, 1985, pp. 57–58, 342–344.

3. Ruth Benedict, *Patterns of Culture*, Boston: Houghton Mifflin, 1961. Reprinted Mariner Books, 2006, p. 2.

4. Robert Pirsig, *LILA: An Inquiry into Morals*, New York: Bantam, 1992, reprint edition, p. 393.

5. Ibid, p. 390. (Quote from Clyde Kluckohn.)

6. Robert Pirsig, *Zen and the Art of Motorcycle Maintenance*. New York: William Morrow, 1974, p. 82.

7. Jon Winoker, *Zen to Go*, Seattle: Sasquatch Books, 2005, p. 84. (Quote from Joseph Campbell.)

8. For some great reading on the subject of feeling and believing we're "right," I'd suggest two books: Robert A. Burton, *On Being Certain: Believing You Are Right Even When You're Not*, New York: St. Martin's Press, 2008; and Jonathan Haidt, *The Righteous Mind: Why Good People Are Divided by Politics and Religion*, New York: Pantheon Books, 2012.

9. Cordelia Fine, *A Mind of Its Own*, New York: W. W. Norton, 2006, p. 13.

10. Charles Ornstein, "Tale of Last 90 Minutes of Woman's Life," *Los*

Angeles Times Online, May 20, 2007, http://articles.latimes
.com/2007/may/20/local/me-king20.

11. Cordelia Fine, *A Mind of Its Own*, New York: W. W. Norton, 2006, p. 2.

12. Tom Robbins, *Still Life with Woodpecker*, New York: Bantam, 2003, p. 85.

Chapter 7

1. Chris Argyris and Donald A. Schön, *Organizational Learning: A Theory of Action Perspective*. Reading, MA: Addison-Wesley, 1978, pp. 3, 20, 144.

2. James D. Murphy, *Flawless Execution: Use the Techniques and Systems of America's Fighter Pilots to Perform at Your Peak and Win the Battles of the Business World*, New York: Harper Business, 2005.

3. Peter M. Senge, *The Fifth Discipline*. New York: Doubleday Currency, 1990, p. 178.

4. William Langewiesche, "Columbia's Last Flight," *Atlantic Monthly*, November 2003, p. 72.

5. Ibid., p. 73.

6. Ibid., p. 72.

7. Cordelia Fine, *A Mind of Its Own*. New York: W. W. Norton, 2006, pp. 108–109.

8. Tom Robbins, *Wild Ducks Flying Backward*, New York: Bantam, 2005, p. 115.

9. *Bridge on the River Kwai*. Directed by David Lean, Columbia Pictures, 1957. Film.

10. Robert Kegan and Lisa Laskow Lahey, *How the Way We Talk Can Change the Way We Work: Seven Languages for Transformation*, San Francisco: Jossey-Bass, 2002, p. 83.

11. Joe Flower, "A Conversation with Ronald Heifetz: Leadership without Easy Answers," 38/4, 1995.

12. Benjamin Akande, personal interview, September 7, 2012.

Chapter 8

1. Jeffrey Schwartz and Sharon Begley, *The Mind and the Brain*, New York: Harper Collins, 2002.

2. For an excellent overview of this subject, I'd suggest *The Mind and*

the Brain (cited in note 1) as well as: *You Are Not Your Brain* by Jeffrey Schwartz and Rebecca Gladding, New York: Penguin, 2011; and *Train Your Mind Change Your Brain*, also by Schwartz and Gladding, New York: Ballantine Books, 2007.

3. John Cusack, "The Alchemists: A Conversation with Phil Stutz, Part III," *The Huffington Post*, July 11, 2012, http://www.huffingtonpost .com/john-cusack/the-alchemists-a-conversa_b_1665825.html.

4. Chris Argyris refers to this as the difference between our "espoused theories" and our "theories-in-use." See also Robert Putnum, Diana McLain Smith, and Chris Argyris, *Action Science*, San Francisco: Jossey-Bass, 1985, pp. 81–82, 89, 92, 98, 156, 243, 245.

5. M. Scott Peck, *The Road Less Traveled*, New York; Simon & Schuster, 1978, p. 31.

6. Susan L. Smalley and Diana Winston, *Fully Present*, New York: Oxford University Press, 2004, p. xvi.

7. Pauline W. Chen, MD, "Teaching Doctors to Be Mindful," *New York Times Online: Well*, October 27, 2011, http://well.blogs.nytimes .com/2011/10/27/teaching-doctors-to-be-mindful/.

8. Ibid.

9. Erich Fromm, *The Art of Being*, New York: Continuum, 1992, p. 23.

10. Frank Barrett, *Yes to the Mess: Surprising Leadership Lessons from Jazz*, Boston: Harvard Business Review Press, 2012. Also from private conversations with Frank, a close colleague and friend with whom I've worked for over 10 years.

11. Ibid.

12. Miles Davis, quoted in Susan Adams, "Leadership Lessons from the Geniuses of Jazz," *Forbes*, November 12, 2012, http://www.forbes .com/sites/susanadams/2012/08/10/leadership-lessons-from-the-geniuses-of-jazz/

Chapter 9

1. Heifetz and Sanders refer to routine problems as "technical" problems. See Riley Sinder and Ronald Heifetz, "Political Leadership: Managing the Public's Problem Solving," *The Power of Public Ideas*, edited by Robert Reich, Cambridge, MA: Harvard University Press, 1990, pp. 179–203.

2. Ronald Heifetz, *Leadership without Easy Answers*, Cambridge, MA: Harvard-Belknap Press, 1994.

3. Ronald Heifetz, *Leadership without Easy Answers*. Cambridge, MA:

Harvard–Belknap Press, 1994, p.184. See also Arnold M. Howitt and Herman B. Leonard, "Dutch," in "The Eye of the Storm: Helping Education Leaders Meet the Challenge of Dealing with Disasters," http://www.hks.harvard.edu/var/ezp_site/storage/fckeditor/file/pdfs/centers-programs/programs/crisis-leadership/eye_storm.pdf

4. Dean Williams, *Real Leadership*, San Francisco: Berrett-Koehler, 2005, p. 7.

5. Jim Collins, *Good to Great*, New York: Harper Business, 2001, p. 88.

6. Ibid.

7. Tom Richman, "Leadership Expert Ronald Heifetz," Inc.com, http://www.inc.com/magazine/19881001/5990.html

8. Chris Argyris, *Overcoming Organizational Defenses*, Boston: Allyn and Bacon, 1990, p. 42.

9. Richard Feynman, *What Do You Care What Other People Think?* New York; W.W. Norton, 1988, p. 117.

10. Gardiner Morse, "Health Care Needs a New Kind of Hero," *Harvard Business Review*, April 2010, http://hbr.org/2010/04/health-care-needs-a-new-kind-of-hero/ar/1

11. William C. Taylor, "The Leader of the Future," *FastCompany.com*. Fast Company, May 31, 1996, http://www.fastcompany.com/37229/leader-future

12. Ibid.

13. For a thorough exploration of the subject of adaptive leadership, I'd highly recommend two books: Ronald Heifetz, *Leadership without Easy Answers*, Cambridge, MA: Harvard-Belknap Press, 1994; and Dean Williams, *Real Leadership*, San Francisco: Berrett-Koehler, 2005.

14 Ronald Heifetz, *Leadership without Easy Answers*, Cambridge, MA: Harvard-Belknap Press, 1994, p. 2.

15 Ibid. p. 20.

16. Gardiner Morse, "Health Care Needs a New Kind of Hero," *Harvard Business Review*, April 2010, http://hbr.org/2010/04/health-care-needs-a-new-kind-of-hero/ar/1

17. Joe Flower, "A conversation with Ronald Heifetz: Leadership without Easy Answers." *The Healthcare Forum Journal* 38/4, July-August 1995.

18. I am using the word "bullshit" in the strict philosophical sense outlined by the eminent moral philosopher Harry G. Frankfurter in his

groundbreaking text *On Bullshit*, Princeton, NJ: Princeton University Press, 2005.

Conclusion

1. Michael Toms, *An Open Life: Joseph Campbell in Conversation with Michael Toms*, New York: Harper & Row, 1989, p. 23.
2. Joseph Campbell, *The Hero with a Thousand Faces*, third edition, Novato, CA: New World Library, 2008.

Index